D0563101

ANTIQUE BAKERY

7

By

Fumi Yoshinaga

DMP
DIGITAL MANGA PUBLISHING

KEIICHIRO TACHIBANA

32 YEARS OLD. OWNER OF THE BAKERY "ANTIQUE." GRANDSON OF THE WEALTHY DIRECTOR OF A MAJOR FINANCIAL GROUP. FORMERLY A TOP-CLASS BUSINESSMAN AT A TRADING COMPANY, HE SUDDENLY QUITS HIS JOB TO START UP THE BAKERY "ANTIQUE." CRYPTICALLY, HE CARES NOT ONE OUNCE FOR ANY SORT OF PASTRY, AND HIS ONLY OPINION OF SWEETS IS, "TASTES LIKE SUGAR." ALTHOUGH HE WAS THE VICTIM OF A KIDNAPPING AT THE AGE OF NINE, HE RETAINS NO MEMORY OF THE EXACT EVENTS OF THE ORDEAL. THE PERPETUAL STUBBLE ON HIS FACE IS SOMETHING HE WAS NOT ALLOWED IN HIS DAYS AS A CORPORATE BUSINESSMAN, AND HE TREASURES ITS PRESENCE AS A SYMBOL OF "A MAN'S AESTHETIC."

EIJI KANDA

21 YEARS OLD. ASSISTANT PASTRY CHEF AT THE BAKERY "ANTIQUE." FORMERLY A MIDDLE STRAW-WEIGHT WORLD CHAMPION BOXER OF GENIUS, HE IS FORCED TO GIVE UP THE RING WHEN HE IS DIAGNOSED AS HAVING DETACHED RETINAS. SHORTLY THEREAFTER, HE ENCOUNTERS ONO'S DEVILISHLY DELICIOUS "CAKE OF ALL CAKES" AND BECOMES AN APPRENTICE PÂTISSIER. DATING BACK TO HIS DAYS AS A BOXER, HE POSSESSES AN INSATIABLE LOVE OF PASTRIES. AN ABANDONED CHILD AS WELL AS A FORMER MEMBER OF A BIKER GANG, HE HAS THE MOST COLORFUL PAST OUT OF THE FOUR MEN, DESPITE HIS YOUNG AGE OF 21.

character

CHIKAGE KOBAYAKAWA

34 YEARS OLD. BECAUSE HIS MOTHER WAS A LIVE-IN HOUSEKEEPER AT THE TACHIBANA RESIDENCE, CHIKAGE HAS KNOWN TACHIBANA SINCE CHILDHOOD. CLUMSY AND A LITTLE SLOW ON THE UPTAKE, HE IS SOMETHING OF A BURDEN. AT THE REQUEST OF TACHIBANA'S CONCERNED PARENTS, HE ARRIVES AT THE BAKERY "ANTIQUE" TO LOOK AFTER TACHIBANA. BECAUSE OF HIS WEAK EYESIGHT AND NERVOUSNESS, HE IS NEVER WITHOUT HIS SUNGLASSES. ONCE HIS GLASSES ARE REMOVED, HIS HANDSOME LOOKS CAPTIVATE ONO, AND ALTHOUGH NEARLY OVERPOWERED BY THE NOTORIOUS "DEMONIC CHARM," CHIKAGE MANAGES TO REMAIN INNOCENT AND OBLIVIOUS - FOR THE TIME BEING!

YUSUKE ONO

32 YEARS OLD. PASTRY CHEF AT THE BAKERY "ANTIQUE." FORMER HIGH SCHOOL CLASSMATES WITH TACHIBANA. TACHIBANA WAS THE OBJECT OF ONO'S FIRST CONFESSION OF LOVE, AS WELL AS HIS FIRST REJECTION. WHEN THE TWO NEXT MEET AGAIN, ONO HAS OVERCOME THIS PAINFUL PAST AND BLOSSOMED INTO A "GAY OF DEMONIC CHARM" WHO IS ABLE TO SEDUCE ANY MAN HE WANTS. ALTHOUGH HE POSSESSES IMPECCABLE TASTE AND TECHNIQUE AS A PASTRY CHEF OF GENIUS, HIS PERSONAL ALLURE IS ALWAYS THE CAUSE OF ROMANTIC TROUBLE IN THE WORKPLACE, AND HE IS FIRED FROM STORE AFTER STORE UNTIL HE FINALLY SETTLES IN AT THE BAKERY "ANTIQUE."

The Story so far...

In the middle of a residential district sits the antique bakery. Tachibana, the owner with the perpetual stubble on his face, and Ono, the genius pastry chef of "Gay Demonic Charm," are former classmates from high school, where Tachibana once brutally rejected Ono's confession of love for him. Kanda, the apprentice pastry chef, is a retired former boxer who possesses a fanatical sweet tooth. Now, a fourth man has arrived on the scene: extremely klutzy and addressing Tachibana as, "My Lord," his name is Chikage Kobayakawa... to these four men at the bakery "antique," customers come to buy their cakes, each with their own story...

Translation	**Sachiko Sato**
Lettering	**Wilbert Lacuna**
Graphic Design	**Eric Rosenberger**
Editing	**Stephanie Donnelly**
Editor in Chief	**Fred Lui**
Publisher	**Hikaru Sasahara**

English Edition Published by
DIGITAL MANGA PUBLISHING
A division of DIGITAL MANGA, Inc.
1487 W 178th Street, Suite 300
Gardena, CA 90248

www.dmpbooks.com

First Edition: February 2006
ISBN: 1-56970-944-0

1 3 5 7 9 10 8 6 4 2

Printed in China

RECIPE 11 pt.1

GOOD EVENING. IT'S FIVE O'CLOCK AND TIME FOR "THE ULTRA NEWS."

TAKE, FOR EXAMPLE, YOKO GONDO ON EVE-NINGS AT FIVE, OR HIROSHI KUNO ON THE NIGHTLY NEWS AT TEN.

THE TIME IS 9:54 P.M., AND THIS IS "THE NEWS TERMINAL." FIRST, OUR TOP STORY...

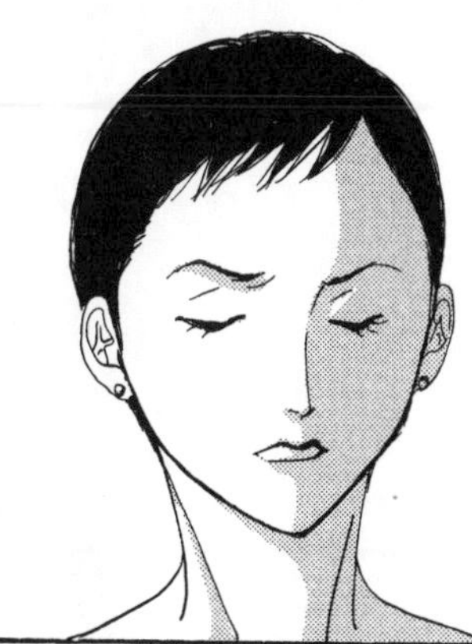
THIS IS NOT THE LIFE I WAS AIMING FOR.

WELL, IT'S ONE OF THOSE DEEP, PHILOSOPHICAL FILMS THAT YOU LOVE, MR. TSUKUDA. BUT I HATE THOSE!
I KNEW YOU WERE GOING TO SAY SOMETHING LIKE THAT, OMUGI! BUT THIS FILM...
OR TETSUYA TSUKUDA AT 11 P.M., DISCUSSING UPCOMING SUMMER MOVIES WITH MOVIE CRITIC OMUGI...THAT WOULDN'T HAVE BEEN SO BAD, EITHER.

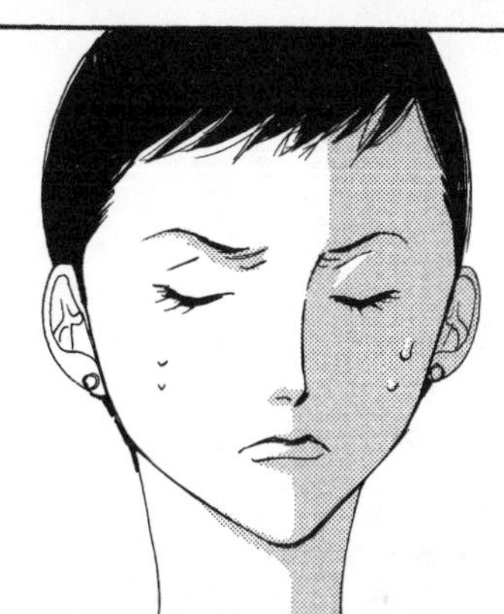
I DIDN'T BECOME AN ANNOUNCER JUST TO BE...TO BE...

ANTIQUE BAKERY
3
...TO BE PART OF SOME FARCICAL REPORTER DUO ASSIGNED ONLY BORDERLINE-COMEDY NEWS, SINGING STUPID SONGS LIKE "BIG-BUSTED FEMALE ANNOUNCER UNIT HARUKA & TAMMY"!!
Recipe 11 (part 1)

AND IT LOOKS LIKE THEY'RE GOING TO LET THE TWO OF US AS A DUO HAVE A REGULAR SEGMENT ON THE FIVE O' CLOCK NEWS.
YEAH...I GUESS I'M A LITTLE HAPPY ABOUT THAT.
YOU'RE A REALIST, AREN'T YOU?
WHAT?

BUT NAKATSU SEMPAI, NOW THAT OUR CD "RUN! FEMALE ANNOUNCERS" HAS BECOME A (TINY) HIT, WE'VE STARTED GETTING SOME (TINY) ROYALTIES, TOO.
I CAN'T STAND IT! IF I CONTINUE WITH THIS STUPID ACT, PRETTY SOON I BET I WON'T EVEN BE ABLE TO RECALL THE NAME OF JAPAN'S CURRENT PRIME MINISTER!!
REMOVING MAKE-UP.
わぁ!!
WAAH!!

NEWS PLUS 5
ニュース
プラス
TA DA DA
TUM TAAM

NO WAY!!

TAMMY'S ♥

HARUKA! AND...

AND NOW FOR TODAY'S SPECIAL REPORT. MISS NAKATSU, MISS KAGAMI?

YES! TODAY WE BRING YOU OUR SPECIAL REPORT FROM THE XYZ SHOPPING DISTRICT, OTHERWISE KNOWN AS THE "SUPER DISCOUNT SHOPPING DISTRICT," WHERE A SECTION OF TUNA IS ONLY AN ASTOUNDING 198 YEN! ISN'T THAT GREAT? IF IT'S TUNA, I'D DEFINITELY WANT TO EAT A ZUKEDON (MARINATED TUNA ON RICE)!

"BARGAINS FOR HOUSEWIVES" REPORT!!

TA TA DA DA DA

TA DA DA DUM

I'D WANT NEGIMA (TUNA WITH SCALLIONS)! AND LATER WE'LL SHOW YOU HOW TO TRANSFORM REGULAR RED-MEAT TUNA INTO TORO (FATTY PREMIUM TUNA)!

I SEE... I THOUGHT SO...I KNEW IT WOULD BE SOMETHING LIKE THIS...

HAAAA... WHAT USE IS FLAUNTING OUR D-CUPS TO A BUNCH OF HOUSEWIVES PREPARING DINNER? KAGAMI, WHAT WAS IT WE'RE SUPPOSED TO BE COVERING TODAY?
IT SEEMS THE HOUSEWIVES LIKE US BECAUSE, DESPITE OUR SEXY IMAGE, WE TALK ABOUT REALLY ORDINARY, DOMESTIC THINGS. STARTING TODAY, WE'RE PROVIDING FULL COVERAGE ON THE SPECIAL LIMITED OPENING OF FAMOUS CAKE SHOPS AT THE BAKERY FAIR IN THE DEPARTMENT STORE SUB-LEVEL FOOD COURT.
I SEE...WE'RE ALWAYS INTERVIEWING OLD MEN AND OLD LADIES WHEN WE COVER THE FISHMONGERS AND VEGETABLE VENDORS. I JUST HOPE THERE'LL BE SOME HANDSOME MEN AT THIS CAKE SHOP THING...
A PLEASURE TO MEET YOU. MY NAME IS TACHIBANA - I'M THE OWNER.

I-I'M ONO, THE PÂTISSIER...

THERE HE IS!!

OH, WOW - HE'S GORGEOUS! HE'S REALLY, **REALLY** GORGEOUS!!

HEH!

YOUR SHOP IS TO BE THE ONLY ONE IN THIS "NISETAN DEPARTMENT STORE SUB-LEVEL'S DREAMY DEBUT OF FAMOUS BAKERIES FAIR" WHICH STARTS THIS APRIL 26TH, WHERE CUSTOMERS WILL BE ABLE TO DINE IN, IS THAT CORRECT?

NOT YOU! I'M TALKING ABOUT THE SHY-LOOKING ONE WITH THE GLASSES! HE'S JUST MY TYPE!!

YES. OUR AIM IS TO PRESENT THE CUSTOMERS WITH THE MOST ELEGANT DESSERTS SUCH AS WOULD BE FITTING FOR THE FINALE OF ANY FINE FULL-COURSE FRENCH MEAL.

HE LOOKS SO TIMID, I BET HE WOULD WALK THREE STEPS BEHIND HIS GIRLFRIEND RATHER THAN RISK EVEN STEPPING ON HER SHADOW - HE'S LOVELY!

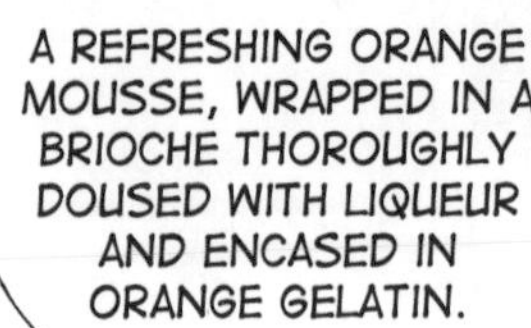
A REFRESHING ORANGE MOUSSE, WRAPPED IN A BRIOCHE THOROUGHLY DOUSED WITH LIQUEUR AND ENCASED IN ORANGE GELATIN.

OHH, IT LOOKS SO TOTALLY DELICIOUS....
WOULD YOU CARE FOR A TASTE?

...

AND ON TOP OF THAT...

...HE'S SO INNOCENT THAT HE HAS TO TURN HIS EYES AWAY FROM MY CHEST! HOW SWEET! WHAT A DIFFERENCE FROM MOST JERKS WHOSE GAZE JUST SCREAMS, "I'M LOOKING, I'M LOOKING," STARING AT MY BOOBS WITHOUT ONCE BOTHERING TO LOOK ME IN THE FACE! I'M SO MOVED!
AH, YES. FOR THIS TIME OF YEAR, I RECOMMEND THIS "VALENCIA".
DAMN, SHE'S GOT A NICE RACK...
I'M SCARED... HER BREASTS ARE LIKE MELONS...
SOOO... CAN YOU TELL US ABOUT YOUR BEST, MOST DELICIOUS CAKE?
I'M LOOKING, I'M LOOKING...

WHAAAT~?! MAY I REEAALL~YY?!
SURRRE, BE MY GUEEEST!
STYLIZED BEAUTY.

THIS IS THE VALENCIA. THE OTHER IS THE POIRES VIN ROUGE-- A TARTE MADE FROM A COMPOTE OF WESTERN PEARS STEWED IN RED WINE, PLACED ATOP A CHOCOLATE-FLAVORED CRUST.
BOTH ARE PRESENTED WITH SOME VANILLA ICE CREAM.

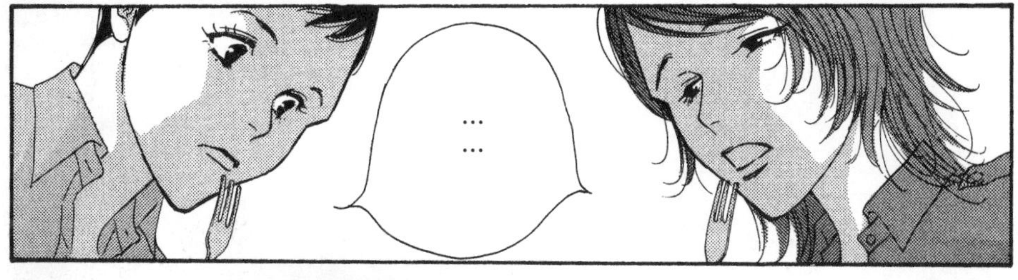
......

じたばたじたばた
FLAP FLAP FLAP FLAP
.....
BOING BOING
BOING BOING
WHY...WHY IS THAT WOMEN ARE SO QUICK TO BREAK INTO DANCE...?
BUT, OH, THEY'VE GOT NICE RACKS...

DEE-
-LICIOUS!! IT'S LIKE - A FIRST? A TASTE SENSATION? HUH? I DON'T KNOW IF THIS WORD CAN BE USED TO DESCRIBE A PASTRY, BUT THE WORD THAT COMES TO MIND IS... "SEXY"!! ♥
IN OTHER WORDS, IT'S A "MATURE" TASTE! BUT IT REALLY IS SUPER-DELISH. WE'LL BRING SOME BACK FOR EVERYONE IN THE STUDIO, OKAAY??

MR. ONO! DON'T RUN AWAY -- I WANT SOME SHOTS OF YOU WORKING. IS IT OK IF I SHOOT FOOTAGE IN HERE?
STILL?!
HAD ESCAPED TO THE KITCHEN...

URGH...!
FLINCH!

OH, WOULD IT BOTHER YOU?! I'M SORRY! OF COURSE, YOU MUST HAVE SPECIAL SECRET RECIPES AND THINGS THAT YOU DON'T WANT ANYBODY TO SEE! I'M SO SORRY!
UM, NO NO! IT'S NOT THAT... IT'S JUST...
HOW DARE I!

UMM... MAY I WATCH, TOO?

JUST ...?

...JUST THAT IT MAKES ME NERVOUS SINCE I'VE NEVER WORKED IN FRONT OF SUCH A BEAUTIFUL LADY BEFORE...
LIAR...

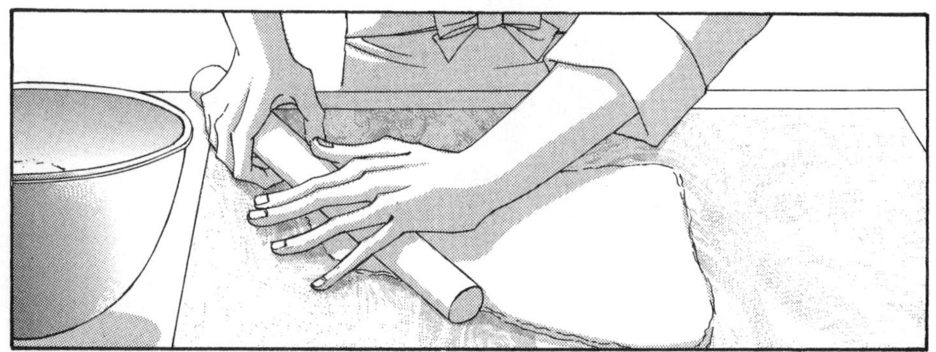

EVEN HIS SKIN IS MORE BEAUTIFUL THAN MINE - OH, IT'S GIVING ME A COMPLEX! I MEAN, MY SCHEDULE IS SO ERRATIC BECAUSE OF WORK AND EVERY-THING, SO...!!

...AND LOOK AT HIS BEAUTI-FUL HANDS!

OH, WHAT A HAND-SOME PROFILE...
...

HUH? IS HE NERVOUS? BECAUSE OF MY BEAUTY?! MY BEAUTY?! IS IT MY BEAUTY?!
I'M SORRY, I'M SORRY! MY HAND SLIPPED, AND...
OH!!
CRASH!

RECORDING IN FIVE SECONDS... 4, 3, 2 -

KAGAMI! YOU CAN HAVE THE KID OR THE STUBBLY GUY, BUT GIVE ME THE ONE IN GLASSES!

GOTCHA!

HUH?! WHAT'S WITH THE GENEROUS ATTITUDE?

♫ TADADADA TADADA ETC. ♫

BOPPA BATTA BATTA!

JUST WHEN I HAVE TO SNEEZE WE'RE BACK FROM COMMERCIAL, WHAT TO DO, FEMALE ANNOUNCER ~♫
THE SHOOT'S IN THE CAN BUT THEN WE'RE CANCELLED BY A HURRICANE! IT GETS TO BE DEPRESSING, FEMALE ANNOUNCER ~♫
BECAUSE I ALREADY HAVE A BOYFRIEND...

TCH! THAT'S RIGHT... YOU DO, DON'T YOU.
♫ BUT THE SPORTS SEGMENT IS PRETTY FUN - AND WITH A LITTLE LUCK, WE MIGHT BAG OURSELVES A RICH MAN ~♫

BUT WE MUST BE WARY OF ILLICIT AFFAIRS, 'CUZ THOUGH WE DON'T MAKE NEARLY AS MUCH AS A CELEBRITY, THE MEDIA'S BASHING IS JUST AS HARSH ♥

♫ RUN RUN RUN, FEMALE ANNOUNCER!

IT DOESN'T MATTER! I'M GOING TO GIVE IT MY BEST FOR THE NEXT TWO DAYS – OH, MR. ONO ♥

GO GO, SEMPAI

THAT WAS SO SCARY...

FOOL! THE COVERAGE IS ONLY FOR TWO DAYS -- TOMORROW'S BOOTH SET-UP AND THE FIRST DAY OF THE FAIR. SUCK IT UP!

CHIKAGE ARRIVES LATE TO AVOID CAUSING ANY TROUBLE.

YOU'RE LUCKY, TACHIBANA... YOU HAD FUN, DIDN'T YOU?

TA-DAH! I GOT TAMMY'S AUTOGRAPH! HER CALLIGRAPHY IS BEAUTIFUL, JUST AS I EXPECTED OF A FEMALE ANNOUNCER.

ALL SHE DID WAS WRITE HER NAME REGULARLY.

BUT ALL THAT ASIDE...WE'RE A SMALL INDEPENDENT BUSINESS, ONO. THERE MAY COME A TIME WHEN YOU'LL HAVE TO INTERACT WITH THE CUSTOMERS, TOO -- YOU CAN'T BE AFRAID OF WOMEN ALL THE TIME. BESIDES, THERE WERE BOTH GIRLS AND BOYS AT OUR SCHOOL AND YOU WERE FINE.
IT MAY NOT SEEM LIKE IT, BUT I'VE ACTUALLY GOTTEN A LITTLE BETTER. AND...MY DISCOMFORT AROUND WOMEN REALLY BEGAN ESCALATING RIGHT AROUND THE TIME I FINALLY BEGAN TO ACCEPT MY HOMOSEXUALITY AND STARTED EXPERIMENTING WITH A LOT OF SEX PLAY.
A LOT OF SEX PLAY?!

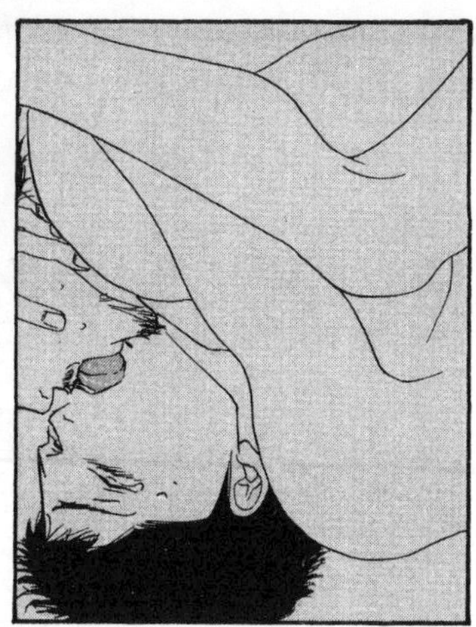

THE FACT THAT I ENJOYED SUCH SLUTTY BEHAVIOR MADE ME REALIZE THAT I REALLY DO HAVE MY MOTHER'S BLOOD FLOWING THROUGH MY VEINS...

OH...NOW I GET IT.
A LOT OF SEX PLAY...

AFTER ALL THIS TIME, I GUESS I STILL HAVEN'T BEEN ABLE TO FORGIVE MY MOTHER...
A LOT OF SEX PLAY...

A LOT OF SEX PLAY...

...SO, THAT'S THE STORY. FOR THE WHOLE WEEK OF THE FAIR, ME AND ONO WILL HAVE TO BE AT THE DEPARTMENT STORE. DURING THAT TIME, I'LL LEAVE YOU GUYS TO MIND THE SHOP, EIJI AND CHIKAGE!

OKAAAY!
...

HEY, EIJI! SINCE THE SHOP'S CLOSED TOMORROW ANYWAY, YOU COME WITH US TO HELP WITH THE SETUP.

HUH?
OH, RIGHT!

...IT WAS WHEN I WAS IN THE FOURTH GRADE.

I WAS WATCHING THE NEWS WITH MY FATHER. I REMEMBER HIM TELLING ME, "THIS BOY IS THE SAME AGE AS YOU, YUSUKE."
"POOR BOY... AN OLDER CHILD LIKE HIM, MISSING FOR TWO WEEKS... IT'S PROBABLY TOO LATE."
SO WHEN KEIICHIRO...TACHIBANA WAS FOUND SAFE, MY FATHER REJOICED AS IF I WERE THE ONE WHO HAD BEEN KIDNAPPED THE WHOLE TIME, REPEATING, "OH, I'M SO GLAD," OVER AND OVER AGAIN.

BUT TACHIBANA WAS HELD CAPTIVE BY HIS ABDUCTOR FOR A WHOLE MONTH. THEY SAY THE STRESS OF AN ORDEAL LIKE THIS IS SO GREAT THAT SOME ADULTS EVEN DEVELOP CANCER AFTERWARD, SO...
...THE AFTERMATH MUST HAVE BEEN DIFFICULT... FOR BOTH TACHIBANA AND HIS RELATIVES.

I'VE NEVER KNOWN MY PARENTS' FACES.

CHIKAGE. YOU'RE NO HELP AT ALL, SO YOU JUST SIT AT HOME.
OKAAAY.
YOU'RE TOO COMPLIANT...

AT MY SECOND ORPHANAGE, I GREW UP WITH BEATINGS. ONE TIME, EVEN THE DIRECTOR OF THE ORPHANAGE CUT ME IN THE CALF WITH A PAIR OF SCISSORS. I'VE COMMITTED EVERY CRIME SHORT OF MURDER, AND THOUGHT I'D SEEN PRETTY MUCH EVERYTHING OF THE DARK SIDE OF THIS WORLD, BUT...

THERE'S ONE THING I REMEMBER ABOUT THE GUY WHO ABDUCTED ME...
HE LOVED CAKE...AND I WAS FED THE CAKE THAT HE BOUGHT, EVERY SINGLE DAY.

EVEN THE GEEZER HAS HIS DARK SECRETS THAT I DON'T KNOW ABOUT...
...PROBABLY...
HEY LOOK, I GOT TAMMY'S AUTO-GRAPH, HEH HEH!
OOH, LUCKY -- PLEASE GET HARUKA'S NEXT TIME!

COME ON, HARUKA! COME STAY AT MY PLACE TONIGHT!

NO, THANK YOU!
AN ENTERTAINER IS A QUESTIONABLE CHOICE FOR A MARRIAGE PARTNER...THEY'RE SO SHALLOW, AND THEIR JOB DOESN'T GIVE THEM A PENSION PLAN. WHAT WILL WE DO IN OUR OLD AGE? OF COURSE IT WOULD BE A DIFFERENT STORY IF HE WERE A **BIG-NAME** CELEB...
キッパリ!!
ZING
HUH?! WHAT'S WITH YOUR SNOTTY ATTITUDE? DON'T THINK YOU'RE SO GREAT JUST BECAUSE YOU GOT SOME BIG TITS -- YOU'RE A BITCHY OLD MAID! AND YOU'RE JUST A ONE-SHOT, ANYWAY!

MRGH
ムカッ!
BUT WE'RE STILL ANNOUNCERS!

HUH ?!

NO WAY! YOU REALLY ARE AN ANNOUNCER?! YOU DON'T LOOK IT!
SHOCK!

OOOH, I HATE THIS JOB! I'M GOING TO HURRY UP AND FIND A MAN SO I CAN QUIT!!
OH, THAT'S RIGHT -- SPEAKING OF MEN, SEMPAI... I'M GOING TO BE GETTING MARRIED TO MINE.
HUH?

HUH?

HUH?
LEFTOVER!

YES! WE'RE HERE AT THE FOOD COURT IN THE FIRST-FLOOR SUB-LEVEL OF NISETAN DEPARTMENT STORE! TODAY, IT'S TIME FOR SETTING UP SHOP, ONE DAY BEFORE THE FAIR BEGINS!

BUSTLE
BUSTLE
bustle
SO, THE GOODS WILL BE DELIVERED AT 9 TOMORROW.
SIR, I'VE GOT THE WRAPPING MATERIAL...
OH -- OVER HERE, OVER HERE!

NOW, WHERE'S OUR BOOTH?
...
BUT NO! I'VE STILL GOT MR. ONO!!
IT'S STILL TOO EARLY TO GET DEPRESSED!!
KEEP UP THE GOOD FIGHT, HARUKA!
SEMPAI?

WHOOA

HUH?
?

HERE...

HE'S HERE...!!

D-DO YOU GET THE FEELING WE'RE BEING NOTICED? OR RATHER, GLARED AT...?
OH!!

THAT'S RIGHT! ONO, HOW MANY OF THESE SHOPS THAT ARE HERE TODAY HAVE YOU WORKED AT?!
A-ABOUT 2/3 OF THEM.
TWO-THIRDS...?! COULD IT BE THAT YOU'RE...?!
I KNOW! DON'T SAY IT!
WHAT? WHAT?

YES, I AM...

THE TROUBLE-MAKER OF THE BAKING INDUSTRY?!

青森りんご

青森りんご

W-WHY? A TROUBLE-MAKER...? BUT ISN'T HE A GENIUS PASTRY CHEF?
YES...NO... IT'S A LONG STORY.

BONK!

NAKAI!!
LET ME GO, BOSS! BECAUSE OF HIM, OUR STORE...
ALL BECAUSE OF THIS HOMO...!!

YOU'RE IN THE WAY! DON'T LIE IN THE MIDDLE OF THE AISLE!!
STOP IT, NAKAI!

WHAT?

WHAT DO YOU THINK YOU'RE DOING TO THE MASTER? AND BESIDES, HE'S NOT A HOMO -- HE'S A ***GAY!!***
KANDA, PLEASE, STOP!
DON'T YELL "GAY" SO LOUD...

GAY...

I'M SORRY. HE'S JUST SO HOT-HEADED...
IT'S QUITE ALL RIGHT. I APOLOGIZE FOR OUR LITTLE RUNT -- HE'S NOTHING BUT TROUBLE.
HEH! WHAT, ARE YOU ANOTHER ONE OF THEM HOMOS?!

WHAT DID YOU CALL ME?! I'M A TRIED-AND-TRUE ***LADIES-MAN***, YOU JERK!
TACHIBANA~!!

I'M SORRY ...!

IT'S FINE...
PLEASE, JUST GO.

IT'S TRUE HE'S TALENTED...HE'S A GENIUS. BUT WHEN TWO OF MY CHEFS BROKE OUT IN A HUGE FIGHT OVER HIM, AND ALL THREE -- ONO INCLUDED -- WERE LET GO AT ONCE, WE STRUGGLED FOR MONTHS TO FIND AND TRAIN THEIR REPLACEMENTS...
SEE! HE DID CAUSE TROUBLE!
THE OWNER OF OUR STORE WAS SMITTEN WITH THIS GUY -- SO WHEN HE WAS DUMPED, IT TOOK FOREVER FOR HIM TO GET OVER IT, AND THE WHOLE STORE SUFFERED!

A PART-TIMER OF OURS GOT INVOLVED WITH HIM. THANKS TO THAT, NO ONE WOULD WORK FOR US BECAUSE A RUMOR GOT AROUND THAT ANYONE WHO WAS EMPLOYED AT OUR STORE WOULD GET SEXUALLY HARASSED BY GAY MEN!

DAMMIT! EVERYONE IS JUST JEALOUS OF THE MASTER'S GENIUS!
I DON'T THINK THAT'S IT...ONO, YOU REALLY...
I'M SORRY...

LEAVE NAKATSU! KAGAMI, GO!
GAY...
SOB
YES! NOW, OVER HERE IS THE BOOTH FOR "ANTIQUE"...

YEAH, THAT'S RIGHT. IT'S LIKE THEY ALWAYS HAVE IN THOSE FOOD COURTS... LIVE DEMONSTRATION! SHOW OFF YOUR SKILLS TO THE GATHERING HOARDS!

UM...THE KITCHEN... CAN BE SEEN... FROM THE OUTSIDE...

TACHI-BANA...
OK, HURRY UP AND BRING IN THE EQUIPMENT.

DEPARTMENT STORE CUSTOMERS... WHICH MEANS...MOSTLY WOMEN...

OR DEAL!

DON'T BE SUCH A WIMP! ALL YOU'RE BASICALLY GONNA BE DOING IS PUTTING THE FINISHING TOUCHES ON PASTRIES THAT HAVE ALREADY BEEN MADE. IT'S NOTHING! YOU'RE A GENIUS PÂTISSIER -- YOU CAN DO IT!
IT'S IMPOSSIBLE, COACH!
I CAN'T! I CAN'T DO IT!! THERE'S NO WAY I CAN WORK WHILE SURROUNDED BY WOMEN...

DON'T WORRY. ALL YOU HAVE TO DO IS WORK ON THE DESSERTS. LEAVE THE ELEGANT HANDLING OF THE THRONG O' FEMALE CUSTOMERS TO ME.
REALLY?! WILL YOU REALLY?!
SO, THIS WAS THE GEEZER'S MOTIVE ALL ALONG...

CHIRP
CHIRP
CHIRP
CHIRP
CHIRP

TH-THEN... THE GREETER FOR TODAY'S FAIR IS...
YES.
ME...
I WILL PROBABLY BE OF NO USE...I'M SORRY.

I GOT A STY IN MY EYE...

ORDEAL!

A WHOLE DAY ALONE AT THE "ANTIQUE" WITH THE GEEZER... WITHOUT THE MASTER...
(A LITTLE) ORDEAL...
OOOHH...THE THRONGING FEMALE CUSTOMERS...
AND BIG-BREASTED REPORTERS...

WOULD YOU MIND REMOVING THEM?
IT'S A LITTLE QUESTIONABLE TO HAVE A WAITER WHO IS WEARING SUNGLASSES, YOU SEE.
NISETAN CHIEF PLANNER
KYOICHI FURUTA

BUT, UM...UM... I ALWAYS... ALWAYS....
BUT WE'RE INDOORS.
IS IT REALLY A PROBLEM? HIS EYES ARE WEAK AGAINST THE LIGHT, AND HE HAS TO WEAR THEM DURING THE DAY...
AS LONG AS YOU ARE ONE OF THE PARTICIPATING VENDORS AT OUR DEPARTMENT STORE, I CANNOT CONDONE ANY ACTION THAT MAY BE CONSTRUED AS AN INSULT TO THE CUSTOMER.

GAH...!!

WHAT THE HELL...? WHY ARE YOU CROAKING LIKE A STRANGLED FROG?!
← BREAK-FAST...
IT KEEPS SEPARATING...

NO MATTER HOW MANY TIMES I TRY, THE RASPBERRY PURÉE AND THE BUTTER KEEP SEPARATING! I'M FOLLOWING THE MASTER'S RECIPE EXACTLY, BUT...

...IT'S NOT COMBINING.
WHAT?! BUT THAT'S A LIMITED-TIME SEASONAL PASTRY WE'RE OFFERING-- A SIGNATURE ITEM OF OUR STORE! DO SOMETHING...! ISN'T THERE ANYTHING WRITTEN IN ONO'S...?

"CONGRATULATIONS, NAKATSU SEMPAI... I HEARD YOU MADE IT IN TO TELE-NICHI..."

"OH, IT'S NOTHING TO BE CONGRATULATED ABOUT-- AFTER ALL, IT'S JUST A COMMERCIAL BROADCASTING STATION. AND IT'S THE SAME TELE-NICHI THAT'S COMMONLY CALLED "THE VARIETY SHOW CHANNEL," YOU KNOW? ≶SIGH≶

...THE REASON THEY REJECTED ME AT NHK MUST BE BECAUSE OF MY EXTREME BEAUTY AND LARGE BREASTS, BOTH MORE WORTHY FOR A MODEL IN A PHOTO MAG THAN A NEWSCASTER...THAT KIND OF THING CAN BE A MINUS FOR AN ANNOUNCER'S IMAGE, YOU KNOW? BECAUSE IT DOESN'T MAKE YOU LOOK INTELLIGENT, SEE? BUT OF COURSE I COULD NEVER BECOME THE TYPE OF WORKAHOLIC CAREER WOMAN WITH HARD EYES AND NO SHRED OF FEMININITY LEFT IN HER, EITHER!"

"REALLY~? YOU COULDN'T BE A CAREER WOMAN, SEMPAI?"

"WELL, I'M OFTEN MISTAKEN FOR ONE BECAUSE OF MY INTELLIGENCE, BUT INSIDE, I'M JUST AN ORDINARY, FEMININE GIRL. OF COURSE, MY OBVIOUS TALENT SHOWS THROUGH NO MATTER HOW I TRY TO HIDE IT, SO IF IT HAPPENS TO LAND ME A JOB AS A NEWSCASTER THEN I WOULD HAVE NO CHOICE BUT TO ACCEPT...BUT EVEN THEN, I WOULD HANDLE MY WORK AS NATURALLY AND ELEGANTLY AS I COULD. WITH MY YOUTHFUL FACE AND CUTE LOOKS, SOME YOUNG EXECUTIVE WILL PROBABLY GET HOOKED ON ME--AND IF HE SHOULD SAY TO ME, 'THERE ARE MANY WOMEN WHO CAN BECOME THIS STATION'S ANNOUNCER, BUT THERE IS ONLY ONE WOMAN IN THE WORLD WHO CAN BECOME MY WIFE,'

THEN I WOULD BE FORCED TO RETIRE FOR MARRIAGE...AT THE VERY LEAST, I WOULD NEVER WANT TO BE A WOMAN OVER 28 CONTINUING TO WORK SIMPLY BECAUSE SHE CAN'T FIND A MAN!"

...

NO PLANS FOR MARRIAGE. CURRENTLY 28 YEARS OLD

SOON-TO-BE MARRIED. CURRENTLY 27 YEARS OLD

AND NOW, HERE IT IS - THE OPENING DAY OF THE FAIR!

ALL STAFF MEMBERS: IT IS NOW TEN MINUTES BEFORE OPENING. PLEASE REPORT TO YOUR VARIOUS SALES STATIONS. THANK YOU!
Recipe 11 (part 2)

I WAS A FRESHMAN IN HIGH SCHOOL.

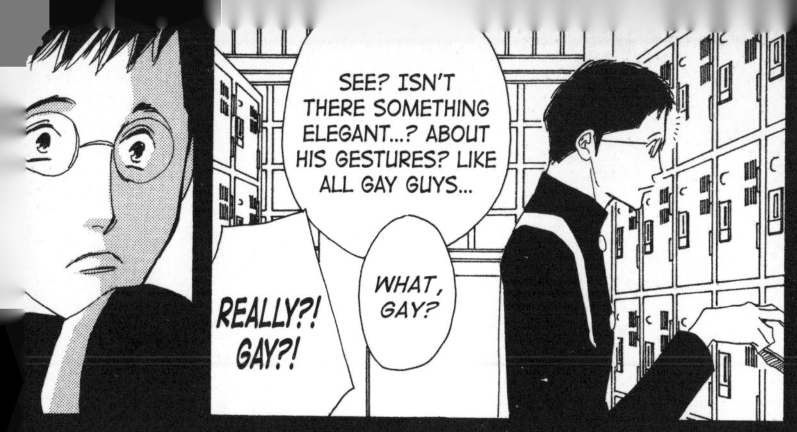
SEE? ISN'T THERE SOMETHING ELEGANT...? ABOUT HIS GESTURES? LIKE ALL GAY GUYS...
WHAT, GAY?
REALLY?! GAY?!

OMIGOD~!!
どっ!!
BWAHAHA

I CAN'T BELIEVE YOU SAID IT SO LOUD!
THAT WAS CLOSE! HAHA HAHA
I TOTALLY JUMPED.

HAHA HAHA

BLUSH!!

OH, NO...JUST REMEMBERING MAKES ME WANT TO CRY...
MR. ONO...

I CAN'T DO IT. I'M NERVOUS ENOUGH AROUND PEOPLE AS IT IS...BUT WITHOUT MY SUNGLASSES, MR. ONO, I'M...I'M...!

...
I WANT TO MAKE HIM CRY SOME MORE, MAKE HIM CLASP HIS ARMS AROUND ME AND MOAN AND GROAN AND...
NO, NO, NO!
THAT'S RIGHT... I MUST BE STRONG. MR. CHIKAGE IS MORE TROUBLED BY THIS THAN I AM. I'VE GOT TO DO SOMETHING!

UM!
THOSE EARRINGS... THEY'RE NOT PIERCED -- THEY'RE CLIP-ONS, RIGHT?
HUH...? Y-YES, BUT...
MAY I BORROW JUST THE ONE ON THE RIGHT?!

PLEASE!!

...WE'VE GOT NO CHOICE.

EIJI, GO DOWN TO SHINJUKU...ASK ONO DIRECTLY. THE DÉLICE AU FRAMBOISE MAY NOT BE READY IN TIME FOR STORE OPENING, BUT IT CAN'T BE HELPED!
NO... ...
NO! I CAN'T DO THAT!

THE DÉLICE IS A POPULAR ITEM OF OURS. AND IF I WERE A CUSTOMER WHO CAME TO THE STORE AND THE CAKE I WANTED WASN'T HERE, I'D BE MAD, TOO.
I CAN'T LET THE REPUTATION OF THE "ANTIQUE" FALL IN THE MASTER'S ABSENCE. LET ME KEEP TRYING ON MY OWN!
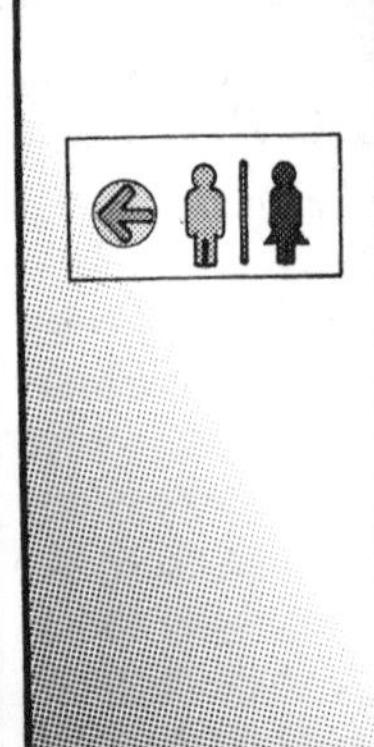

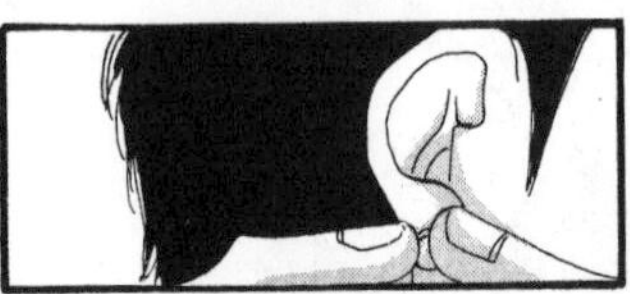
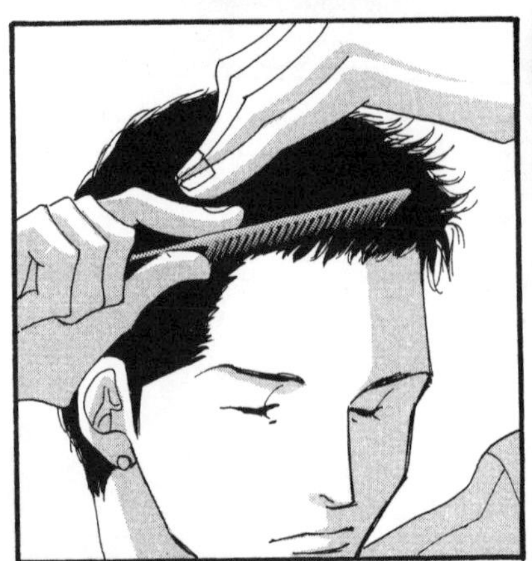

ありがとう
ございました

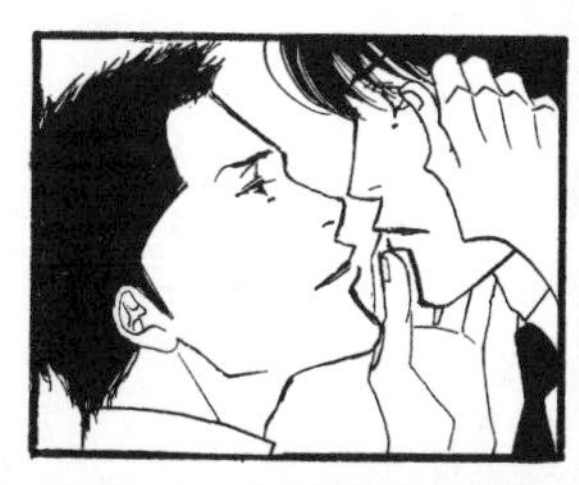

ニコッ
SMILE

IT'S OKAY NOW, MR. CHIKAGE -- DON'T CRY ANYMORE. I'LL TAKE TACHIBANA'S PLACE TODAY!

H-HUH? WHY AM I BLUSHING TOO...?

...

...

HM?

NOW THAT I THINK ABOUT IT, I SEEM TO REMEMBER ONO MENTIONING SOMETHING ABOUT THE PURÉE BEING COLDER THAN THE BUTTER...
WHAT?!

IS *THAT TRUE?!*
I HEARD WHEN I ASKED HIM HOW IT WAS MADE SO I COULD MAKE UP A SPIEL FOR THE CUSTOMERS, I THINK...NO, I'M SURE I HEARD IT!
OKAY! I'LL TRY IT!!
THE ONLY THING I RELY ON YOU FOR IS YOUR MEMORY!
THE ONLY THING?

HEY, KAGAMI.
YES?
I'LL BUY YOU SOME SILK PAJAMAS. LET'S GO UP TO THE SECOND FLOOR LATER AND PICK OUT A CUTE SET.

HUH?
BUT JUST SO YOU KNOW-- I'M BUYING THEM FOR YOUR HUBBY!

CONGRATU-LATIONS, I HOPE YOU'LL BE VERY HAPPY.

OH! FIFTEEN MINUTES AFTER OPENING, IT LOOKS LIKE THE "ANTIQUE" HAS GOT THEIR *FIRST* CUSTOMER!

EXCUSE ME...
YES!
HERE IT GOES!
本日のオスス
THIS "EARLY SUMMER CHOCOLATE PARFAIT À LA ANTIQUE"...HOW IS IT DIFFERENT FROM A NORMAL PARFAIT?
"OK, MR. CHIKAGE? WHEN A CUSTOMER ASKS YOU SOMETHING, DO EXACTLY AS I TELL YOU."

"STARE STRAIGHT INTO THE CUSTOMER'S EYES..."
STARE...
じっ
STARE...

HUH?

"MOVE YOUR FACE IN CLOSE AND SAY IN A HUSHED VOICE, 'ONCE YOU HAVE TASTED IT, YOU WILL UNDERSTAND.'"

ONCE YOU HAVE TASTED IT, YOU WILL UNDERSTAND...

I'LL HAVE IT...!
UM! DOES THAT GO FOR THIS "FAIR-ONLY BUCK-WHEAT-FLOUR CREPE WITH HONEY AND ICE CREAM" TOO?!
YES, ONCE YOU HAVE TASTED IT, YOU WILL UNDER-STAND, MADAM.

THUNK!

IT WORKED, MR. ONO! I DID EXACTLY WHAT YOU TOLD ME TO, AND IT WORKED PERFECTLY! TWO ORDERS -- A PARFAIT AND A CREPE!
SEE? GOT IT, ONE PARFAIT AND A CREPE!

SIZZ...!

SQUEAK!

FLIP!

WOW! HE'S GOOD!

OK, THE PEOPLE I JUST SAW WERE ONLY DRESSED AS WOMEN, AND THEY ARE ACTUALLY BEAUTIFUL MEN. THEY ARE BEAUTI-FUL MEN. THEY ARE BEAUTIFUL MEN...!
SELF-HYPNOSIS...

GRIN!

GOT IT! WHEN THE TEMPERATURE OF THE PUREMAKES THE BOTTOM OF THE BOWL FEEL A LITTLE BIT CHILLY, IT WORKS!

YOU GOT IT?!

YEAH -- THEY MIXED TOGETHER WITHOUT SEPARATING! HANG ON, I'LL START MAKING THE PASTRIES RIGHT AWAY!

LOOKS SO DELICIOUS... ♥
IT'S BEAUTIFUL! THE CREPE IS DRENCHED WITH GOLDEN HONEY LIQUEUR, AND THE PARFAIT -- THE WINE RED OF THE DARK CHERRIES MATCHES THE BURNT UMBER OF THE CHOCOLATE PERFECTLY... THEY LOOK SUPER ULTRA TRÈS DELICIOUS!

HOW DOES IT TASTE?
...
...
...
...

IT MAKES YOU WANT TO FLAP AROUND AND DANCE, DOESN'T IT~?
IT DOES! IT'S SO GOOD, IT SEEMS TO MAKE EVERYONE WANT TO DANCE! IT REALLY DOES MAKE YOU WANT TO DANCE!
...
...!!
...!!
...!!
...!!

UM...
WELCOME. RIGHT THIS WAY.

I KNEW I'D END UP HERE.

DEAR GOD, DEAR BUDDHA, DEAR LADIES-MAN TACHIBANA... PLEASE LEND ME YOUR STRENGTH...!
SMILE!

DÉLICE AU FRAMBOISE... READY!!

SLUNK!

...12 O'CLOCK, ON-THE-DOT!

MADE IT...
WE MADE IT...IT'S OPENING TIME...

CHEEP
CHEEP
CHEEP
CHIRP
CHIRP

CHIRP
CHIRP...

OH!

OHH, HELLO! ARE YOU GOING OUT? YES, DOWN TO YUZAWAYA IN KICHIJOJI!. OH, IS THAT SO?

...HEY.
GEEZER.
HM?
ARE YOU RUNNING A BAKERY 'CUZ YOU'RE TRYING TO CATCH THE GUY WHO ABDUCTED YOU?

CHIRP
CHIRP
CHIRP...

HMMM...
IT'S LIKE...I DON'T...
I DON'T REALLY KNOW HOW TO EXPLAIN IT...

...
SO, THERE ARE SOME THINGS THAT EVEN *YOU* CAN'T EXPLAIN?

SURE.

OH.
YUP.

ONE AFTERNOON TEA SET, YOUR ORDER IS READY!

THANK YOU FOR WAITING. HERE IS YOUR AFTERNOON TEA SET.

ANOTHER ORDER...ONE CREPE AND A THREE-ASSORTMENT PLATTER, PLEASE.
OKAY.

SEE?
YEAH!
OH, IT'S TRUE... AN EAR-RING...

MR. CHIKAGE, MR. CHIKAGE.
COULD YOU COME OVER HERE AND SMILE WITH ME FOR A SECOND?
YES?
HUH?

?

SQUEAL!!
THE AFTERNOON HOUR HAS PASSED INTO EVENING, AND THE POPULARITY OF THESE SHOPS CONTINUES UNABATED! THIS HAS BEEN NAKATSU AND KAGAMI, REPORTING TO YOU FROM THE DELICIOUS CAKE SHOPS IN THE DEPARTMENT STORE SUB-LEVEL!
OH, ANOTHER THREE HIGH-SCHOOL GIRLS JUST WENT IN...

SORRY I KEPT YOU OPEN RIGHT UP UNTIL CLOSING TIME...THE CAKE WAS SO DELICIOUS.
OH NO, IT WAS NO TROUBLE AT ALL. THANK YOU VERY MUCH.
THANK YOU.

TADAA DADA TA DADADA
THANK YOU FOR YOUR PATRONAGE OF NISETAN DEPARTMENT STORE. WE HOPE TO SERVE YOU AGAIN SOON...
TADAA TADA-DADA

...
...

SWOON!
M-MR. ONO?!

I'M ALL RIGHT. IT'S JUST... NOW THAT THE TENSION IS GONE...BUT CAN I STAY LIKE THIS A LITTLE LONGER?
Y-YES.
RUB RUB RUB
GOODY! I GET TO RUB HIS CHEST. OH, THERE'S NOTHING LIKE A MAN'S CHEST TO LEAN ON...

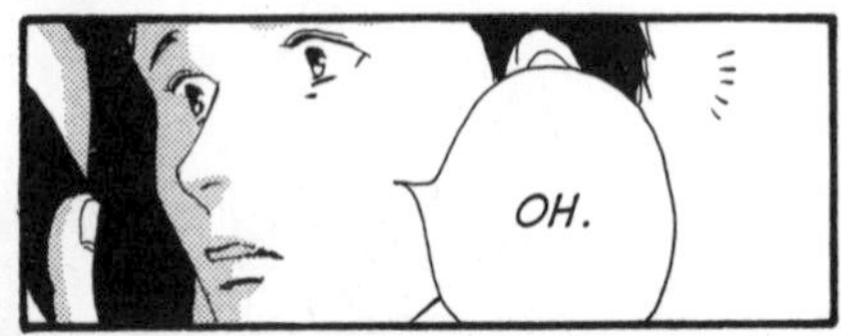
OH.

OH!

THANK YOU SO MUCH! IT REALLY HELPED.
...
I DON'T KNOW HOW TO THANK YOU -- REALLY. REALLY...!

PFT!

HUH?
OH, NOTHING... HAHAHA.
IT'S JUST THAT... NOW YOU'RE SO COMPLETELY DIFFERENT FROM THE ALLURING, CONFIDENT MAN WE SAW JUST MOMENTS BEFORE!

HUH?! ALLURING AND CONFIDENT?! NO, NO! I WAS JUST ACTING SO OBVIOUSLY GAY...! BUT WOMEN SEEM TO FIND THAT SORT OF THING ENTERTAINING, YOU SEE, SO...
HUH? SO OBVIOUSLY GAY? BUT YOU ***ARE*** GAY AREN'T YOU?

IF YOU ARE GAY, THEN WHAT'S WRONG WITH ACTING IT? BUT ALL THAT ASIDE... MAYBE THE FEMALE CUSTOMERS WERE A LITTLE BIT ATTRACTED BY THE "OBVIOUSLY GAY" THING. BUT DO YOU THINK WOMEN BLUSH WHEN THEY WATCH A GAY MAN LIKE, FOR EXAMPLE, THAT MOVIE CRITIC -- OMUGI? THEY DON'T, DO THEY? THE REAL REASON YOU WERE SO POPULAR WITH THE WOMEN TODAY...
...WAS BECAUSE YOU WERE REALLY, REALLY, REEAALLY ATTRACTIVE!

THANK YOU...

OHHHH...I'M SUCH A KIND WOMAN, I'M JUST TOO KIND...! CHEERING UP A MAN WHO WON'T EVER MARRY ME, BUYING PAJAMAS FOR A SNEAKY CO-WORKER WHO'S GOING TO LEAVE ME BEHIND AT WORK TO GO OFF AND GET MARRIED...THIS KINDNESS IS WHAT ALWAYS LEAVES ME HOLDING THE SHORT END OF THE STICK!
HUH? BUT I'M NOT GOING TO BE QUITTING MY JOB.

WHY?!
THIS CRAPPY JOB?! THIS SUPER-BUSY, ERRATIC JOB?! AND ANYWAY, DIDN'T YOU SAY YOU ONLY BECAME AN ANNOUNCER JUST BECAUSE YOU HAPPENED TO GET A POSITION HERE?
UMM ~... MY PARENTS DIED WHEN I WAS IN JUNIOR HIGH...AND I WAS ADOPTED AND RAISED BY MY AUNT AND UNCLE...

OH, BUT MY AUNT AND UNCLE ARE REALLY NICE PEOPLE...I THINK THAT'S ALL THE MORE REASON WHY I WAS SO HAPPY WHEN I GOT THIS JOB ~ ...I WAS LIKE, "OH ~, NOW I'LL BE ABLE TO SUPPORT MYSELF AND NOT BE A BURDEN TO MY AUNT AND UNCLE ~."
SO, EVEN WHEN I GET OLD ~ AND THEY SHUFFLE ME OFF TO SOME WORK IN THE BACKGROUND ~ I INTEND TO KEEP WORKING... I DON'T REALLY CARE WHAT THE JOB IS. I'LL BE HAPPY AS LONG AS I'M ABLE TO EARN MY OWN LIVING...

...
IS IT ME...

...OR DO I SEEM LIKE A COMPLETE JACKASS IN COMPARISON, BITCHING AND TRYING TO ESCAPE MY WORK THROUGH MARRIAGE?! ***WAIT, NOW THAT I'VE SAID IT, I DO LOOK LIKE A JACKASS!!***

WHAT ~? SEMPAI, YOU'RE NOT A JACKASS AT ALL ~. I KNOW YOU LOOK THROUGH THE ENGLISH NEWSPAPERS EVERY DAY JUST SO YOU'LL BE READY WHEN YOU GET TO BE A REAL REPORTER, AND EVEN WHEN NO ONE HAS ASKED, YOU'RE PATIENTLY STUDYING AND KEEPING UP WITH WORLD FINANCIAL AND POLITICAL NEWS ON YOUR OWN ~.

WAIT, SHH! DON'T SAY THAT, I'M KEEPING IT A SECRET! I MEAN, I'M ONLY DOING THIS VARIETY-PROGRAM-ISH JOB SO PEOPLE WILL SCOFF, "WHAT, IS SHE SERIOUSLY AIMING TO BE A NEWS REPORTER?! HA! DON'T MAKE ME LAUGH! I'D NEVER IN A MILLION YEARS MARRY AN AMBITIOUS, CAREER-DRIVEN, THINKS-SHE'S-SO-SMART WOMAN LIKE HER!" AND I DON'T WANT TO HEAR THAT!
WHAAT~? BUT, SO WHAT? WHAT'S WRONG WITH A BIG-BUSTED NEWSCASTER WHO REPORTS THE DAY-TO-DAY TRENDS WITHIN NAGATA CITY~? I THINK YOU'D BE PERFECT, SEMPAI~! AND BESIDES...

...WHAT'S WRONG WITH A COMPETENT WOMAN LOOKING AND ACTING LIKE THE COMPETENT WOMAN SHE IS~? I THINK YOU'RE VERY CHARMING THE WAY YOU ARE, SEMPAI~.

YOU THINK SO?
I THINK SO...
REALLY?
I DO.

THAT'S RIGHT. SO, THE PENIS OF ANY MAN THAT CAN'T APPRECIATE YOUR CHARMS IS...

YOU'RE RIGHT!

NOT WORTHY ENOUGH FOR ME!!
YEAAAH~
THE GUY WHO'S GOING TO MARRY KAGAMI MUST HAVE SOME BIG STONES, TOO...
IN ANY CASE... IN ANY CASE, I WOULD NEVER, EVER CONSIDER EITHER ONE OF YOU TO BE MY WIFE...

SO, THE PLACE YOU FINALLY SETTLED DOWN IN TURNED OUT TO BE A BAKERY OF TRADITIONAL FRENCH PASTRIES... IT SUITS YOU.

TO BE HONEST, WATCHING YOU WORK IS ALWAYS A LESSON IN TECHNIQUE. YOUR PASTRIES LOOK AS GOOD AS ALWAYS. SEE YA.
NAKAI!

UM...
I'VE BEEN WORRIED THIS WHOLE TIME...ABOUT THAT RECIPE FOR THE NEW PRODUCT THAT I WAS TESTING OUT BEFORE I QUIT...IT WAS NEVER COMPLETED...

THE *"AMERICAN BAKED CHEESECAKE WITH WALNUTS."*
THE OWNER AND I -- WE COMPLETED THAT RECIPE ON OUR OWN. JUST AS YOU SAID, THE STRAWBERRY-AND-WHIPPED-CREAM DECORATION ON TOP MADE IT LOOK JUST LIKE SHORTCAKE, AND IT BECAME VERY POPULAR. IT'S NOW ONE OF OUR REGULAR ITEMS.

THAT'S WHEN I REALIZED THAT ALL THE RECIPES WE HAVE LEFT ARE THE ONES *YOU* CREATED.
PERSONALLY, I'M STILL GLAD THAT A TROUBLE-MAKER LIKE YOU LEFT OUR STORE, BUT...
...IT'S ALSO BECAUSE OF YOU THAT OUR STORE HAS BEEN ABLE TO COME THIS FAR.

CHIKAGE! COME ON, CHIKAGE! MY STY CLEARED UP NOW...LET ME TRADE PLACES WITH YOU ON THIS LAST DAY OF THE FAIR, AT LEAST!
NOOO, I LIKE IT THERE! THE CUSTOMERS ARE SO NICE TO ME...
GEEZER! YOU'RE BEING IMMATURE! REALLY IMMATURE!
ACTUALLY, TACHIBANA IS YOUNGER THAN MR. CHIKAGE, BUT...

ASAGAYA PEARL CENTER
阿佐谷 パールセンター
BEEP
BEEEP

ぬっ
LOOM

ぬっ
LOOM
HONK
BRRRM
BUSTLE
BUSTLE

Recipe 12 (part 1)

...
...
SIZZ...

...
...

NEVER MIND THAT HE'S A FOREIGNER-- IT'S THOSE RED ROSES...

NEVER MIND THAT HE'S A FOREIGNER-- IT'S THOSE RED ROSES...

SWISH

SWISH

SWISH

NEVER MIND THAT HE'S A FOREIGNER-- IT'S THOSE RED ROSES...

IT'S SOOO CROWDED!
OH, THEY HAVE BREAD HERE, TOO. LOOKS GOOD.
THE BREAD IS VERY TASTY HERE-ESPECIALLY THE CROISSANTS.
REALLY? MAYBE I'LL BUY ONE.
クロワッサン

ドッ!
THRONG

I'M SO SORRY FOR THE DELAY--THANK YOU FOR WAITING!
THIS "LIMONY" ...WHAT KIND OF CAKE IS IT?
AH YES! THAT IS A CHOCOLATE-AND-LEMON-CREAM CAKE.
OOH... LEMON!

WHAT'S THIS?!
IT'S SO TOTALLY GOOD!!

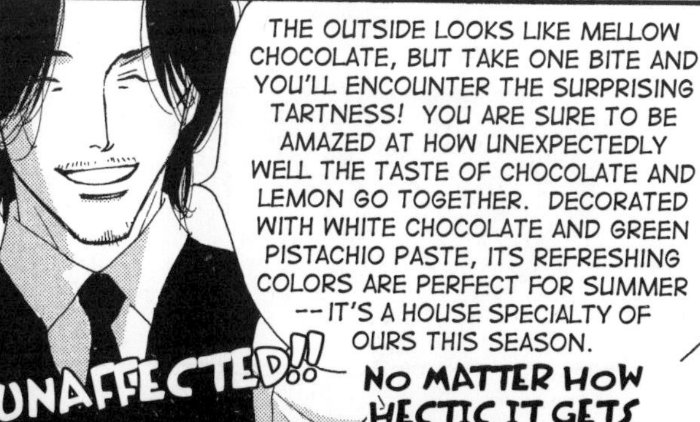
THE OUTSIDE LOOKS LIKE MELLOW CHOCOLATE, BUT TAKE ONE BITE AND YOU'LL ENCOUNTER THE SURPRISING TARTNESS! YOU ARE SURE TO BE AMAZED AT HOW UNEXPECTEDLY WELL THE TASTE OF CHOCOLATE AND LEMON GO TOGETHER. DECORATED WITH WHITE CHOCOLATE AND GREEN PISTACHIO PASTE, ITS REFRESHING COLORS ARE PERFECT FOR SUMMER --IT'S A HOUSE SPECIALTY OF OURS THIS SEASON.
NO MATTER HOW HECTIC IT GETS, THIS MAN IS...
UNAFFECTED!!

HEY, HEY, CHI! THIS CAKE IS REAALLY GOOD!!
ISN'T IT?! ISN'T IT?!
REAALLY~? THEN I WANNA TRY ONE TOO! CHI, ANOTHER LIMONY PLEEAASE.

COMING RIGHT UP!
WE'RE READY HERE, TOO.

OH, YES! YOUR ORDER?
TWO LIMONYS, ONE ICE TEA AND A BLEND.
RIGHT AWAY!

UMM...THAT MEANS...THE NUMBER OF LIMONYS IS...
THREE! THAT'S THREE LIMONYS, CHI!
IT'S ALL RIGHT -- WE'RE IN NO HURRY. YOU JUST TAKE YOUR TIME, DEAR.
...
YES! THANK YOU VERY MUCH!
WAIT, THAT'S NO GOOD...

WHEW! WHAT A THRONG! IT LOOKS LIKE IT'S FINALLY THINNED OUT.

HEH!
HEE HEE HEE HEE HEE!
OHH, I CAN'T STOP SMILING. WE'VE SEEN A 1.5-TIMES SALES INCREASE SINCE WE WERE FEATURED IN THAT "NEWS PLUS 5" SPECIAL!

BEHOLD THE POWER OF MASS MEDIA! LOOK, WE'RE EVEN MENTIONED IN ALL THESE MAGAZINES -- "NANAKO," "TOKYO QUAKER" AND "KATEI JIHO (HOUSEHOLD NEWS)"!
...
SO, ONO...SHOULD OUR SECOND STORE LOCATION BE AOYAMA? IS AOYAMA GOOD? OR MAYBE KICHIJOJI WOULD BE BETTER! WHAT DO YOU THINK?!
GEEZER, YOU'RE DREAMING AGAIN! DREAMING!!
Nanako

WHAT ARE YOU TALKING ABOUT? EVEN THE FAMOUS TARTE SHOP IN DAIKANYAMA IS A BRANCH OF THE MAIN STORE IN SHIZUOKA! WHEN YOU THINK ABOUT IT, IT'S NOT IMPOSSIBLE FOR US, EITHER.
WE'RE TOO SHORT-HANDED! DO YOU KNOW HOW BUSY THE MASTER IS NOW, AS IT IS?!
NO, NO, KANDA - DON'T WORRY ABOUT THAT.
THERE WAS A TIME WHEN I WAS WORKING 18 HOURS, FROM DAWN TO LATE AT NIGHT, AT ABOUT A TENTH OF THE SALARY I'M MAKING NOW. SO COMPARED TO THOSE DAYS...

1/10?!
18 HOURS ?!
YEAH. SO HAVING A HEAVY WORK-LOAD DOESN'T BOTHER ME AT ALL.. BUT...
WHERE WAS THAT, A SLAVE-LABOR BAKERY?!

...I'M STILL MAKING PAYMENTS FOR A DIOR COAT I BOUGHT IN THE WINTER, BUT THE OTHER DAY I SAW THESE PRADA PANTS...SO IF YOU COULD GIVE ME MAYBE A TINY BONUS, TACHIBANA, I'D BE REALLY GRATEFUL...
OH, AND FOR KANDA TOO, OF COURSE.

HUH? BUT I DON'T REALLY NEED IT, MASTER.
OHH...BUT THEN THAT MAKES ME LOOK LIKE I'M THE ONLY ONE THAT'S IN IT FOR THE MONEY!
BUT YOU REALLY *ARE* THE ONLY ONE THAT'S IN IT FOR THE MONEY!

バイバーイ!
BYE BYE!
OK THEN, CHI -- WE'LL COME AGAIN WITH EVERYONE, LIKE WE DID AT CHRIST-MASTIME!
DEEP BOW
WE AWAIT YOUR VISIT.

<EXCUSEZ-MOI.>*
WELCOME!

**NOTE: IN FRENCH*

IS THIS YUSUKE ONO'S SHOP?
WELCOME!
YOU'RE A TALL ONE FOR A JAPANESE... IS THIS YUSUKE'S SHOP?
WELCOME!
WHAT ARE YOU-- A GARÇON OR A BROKEN RECORD? JUDGING FROM YOU AND THE QUALITY OF THE CUSTOMERS THAT JUST LEFT, THIS MUST BE ONE LOUSY SHOP...
EXCUSE ME! THIS IS MY SHOP!!

POOR YUSUKE... STUCK WITH A HICK LIKE YOU. YOU LOOK LIKE YOU'D BE LOUSY AT BOTH SEDUCTION AND SEX. OR DID YOU USE THE PROSPECT OF EMPLOYMENT HERE AS BAIT AND FORCE HIM INTO SLEEPING WITH YOU?
I THOUGHT AT FIRST THAT THIS GARÇON WAS YUSUKE'S NEW MAN, BUT I GUESS I WAS WRONG. YOU MUST BE THE ONE.

HMPH!
KNEW IT WAS A LOUSY SPOT. DO ALL JAPANESE BAKERIES TREAT THEIR CUSTOMERS SO RUDELY?
WHAT CUSTOMER? YOU'RE PROBABLY JUST SOMETHING ONO PICKED UP DOWN ON SECOND AVENUE, RIGHT? IF YOU WANT TO SPEAK TO ONO, COME BACK AFTER CLOSING!

JEAN-BAPTISTE?!
YOU...YOU JUST INJURED MY PRIDE TWOFOLD, THREEFOLD...NO, ***FOURFOLD!!***
......!!

IT *IS* JEAN-BAPTISTE! WHAT ARE YOU DOING HERE IN JAPAN?!

...WHY, I'M HERE TO KNEEL DOWN BEFORE YOU AND DECLARE MY LOVE FOR YOU AGAIN...!

......!!
......!!
......!!
......!!

MY LOVE...!!!

THIS IS JEAN-BAPTISTE HEVENS.
AND...
MY TEACHER IN PASTRY-MAKING.
...PROBABLY ONE OF THE MOST FAMOUS PASTRY CHEFS IN FRANCE. HE'S THE OWNER-CHEF OF THE PÂTISSERIE ***"JEAN-BAPTISTE HEVENS"*** ON RUE SAINT-HONORÉ IN PARIS.

THE...THE MASTER'S TEACHER?! THE ***GRAND-MASTER?!***
THAT MAKES HIM THE TRUE CHAMP AMONG PASTRY CHEFS...I...I... ***WOULD GIVE MY BODY TO HIM!!***
KANDA... JUST SO YOU KNOW... THAT'S NOT A JOKE WITH THIS MAN EITHER...
YUSUKE.

...

COULD YOU BRING ME ONE EACH OF THIS STORE'S CROISSANT, APPLE PIE AND CHOCOLATE ÉCLAIR?

HERE YOU ARE.

OUI, MONSIEUR.

...
...

SHK!
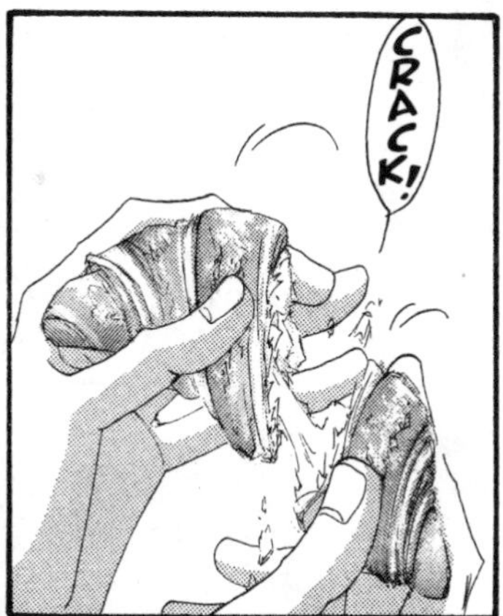
CRACK!

MUNCH!

SSK!

...
...

NOT BAD!

...!

I'M SO GLAD!
OH, WHAT A SMILE! YOU HAVEN'T CHANGED ONE BIT, MY ADONIS...!
GRRRRRR
IF YOU TWO PUT YOUR FACES ANY CLOSER TOGETHER, I'LL HAVE TO *KILL* YOU...!

HAHAHA...WHAT A JEALOUS MAN. YOU'D BETTER BE CAREFUL, OR YUSUKE WILL LEAVE YOU!
HE'S NOT MINE IN THE FIRST PLACE!
HEY, YUSUKE-- I'D LIKE SOME GREEN TEA ICE CREAM. DON'T YOU HAVE GREEN TEA ICE CREAM HERE?

YEAH, RUN BY A JAPANESE! WHERE'S THE BLACK SESAME BLANCMANGE? THE WAFFLES WITH RED BEAN CREAM? THE SOY-POWDER DACQUOISE?
HE MEANS "KINAKO" (SOY-BEAN FLOUR)
OF COURSE WE DON'T! THIS IS A FRENCH BAKERY!
U-UM... YOU TWO?
I CAN'T UNDERSTAND WHAT THEY'RE SAYING...

.....
.....
.....
...
...
...
I CAN'T UNDER-STAND...

T-TOO SIMILAR TO GET ALONG?
I DON'T LIKE THIS GUY!!
OH! THEY'RE SPEAKING IN A FOREIGN LANGUAGE!!
...AND HE JUST GOT IT.

YOUNG EMPEROR OF THE PASTRY WORLD
THE MAGIC OF JEAN-BAPTISTE HEVENS HOTEL MOKURA
"JEAN-BAPTISTE HEVENS FAIR"
7/27 ~ 8/10

時報
家庭時報
特集
名店のパティシ
8
HM?

SO! THAT GUY JUST SWUNG BY AS A SIDE-TRIP. HE'S ACTUALLY IN JAPAN ON BUSINESS...TO HOLD A DESSERT FAIR AT A HOTEL.
"YOUNG EMPEROR OF THE PASTRY WORLD"? WHAT AN EXAGGERATION!
OF COURSE. HE MAY NOT LOOK IT, BUT HE'S A HARDCORE ARTISTE. HE WOULD NEVER LEAVE HIS STORE UNATTENDED WITHOUT GOOD REASON.

NO, IT'S NOT. HE REALLY *IS* A GENIUS.
I'LL NEVER BE AS GOOD AS HE IS...MY SKILLS PALE IN COMPARISON.

YOU MENTIONED BEFORE THAT YOU WENT TO PARIS CHASING AFTER THE MAN YOU LOVED...IS THAT HIM?
OH, NO... THAT WAS A TOTALLY DIFFERENT GUY.
SO HE WAS THE NEXT GUY YOU MET AFTER YOU GOT TO PARIS...?
NO, NOT HIM EITHER. JEAN WAS... LET'S SEE...

......
......
THIS MANY MEN LATER... I THINK?

DIDN'T I TELL YOU? I CAME TO JAPAN TO DECLARE MY LOVE FOR YOU. INVITE ME IN.

?!
WHAT?!

RUSTLE
RUSTLE
RUSTLE
CLICK
THWAP!
I...I WAS SO CONSPICUOUS WITH THESE ROSES...IT WAS A LITTLE EMBAR-RASSING...

LIAR.
I'M ONLY A SIDE-TRIP...YOU CAME ON BUSINESS. I ALREADY KNOW.
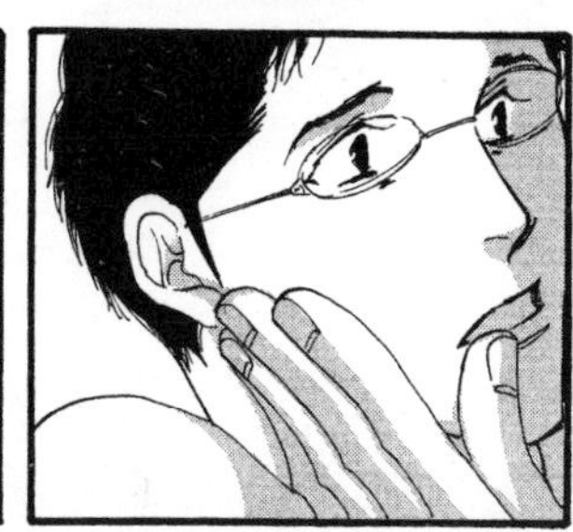

NO, I CAME TO SEE YOU...AND DO BUSINESS ON THE SIDE.

IT DOESN'T MATTER. HURRY AND GET IN BEFORE SOMEONE SEES US...

KLICK..

I'M JUST LETTING YOU KNOW, THE BAKERY BUSINESS IS VERY DEMANDING. WHEN IT GETS BUSY, YOU'LL WORK THROUGH THE NIGHT. ON TOP OF THAT, I'M VERY SHORT-TEMPERED. I'M PRONE TO LASH OUT WITH MY HANDS FIRST, RATHER THAN MY TONGUE.

AND THIS IS A TINY STORE. THE PAY WILL BE HORRIBLE.
TO BE HONEST, SINCE I JUST BECAME INDEPENDENT FROM MY FATHER I HAVEN'T GOT ENOUGH MONEY TO HIRE A PROPER FRENCH APPRENTICE... I THOUGHT A NON-FRENCH-SPEAKING ASIAN WOULD WORK FOR LESS PAY. STILL WANT THE JOB?
I DON'T MIND! I'LL DO ANYTHING IF YOU'LL JUST GIVE ME A POSITION!
REALLY?
YES!
...
OK!
SO, YUSUKE ONO, YOU ARE HIRED. YOU WILL CONSIDER MY ORDERS ABSOLUTE, AND YOUR RESPONSE IS ALWAYS TO BE, "OUI, MONSIEUR."
YOUR RESPONSE?
OUI, MONSIEUR!
WAAH...
I CAN'T HEAR YOU!
OUI, MONSIEUR!
I'D COME HOME FROM SCHOOL, SEE? AND THE FIRST THING I'D ALWAYS DO WAS COUNT HOW MANY TRAYS THERE WERE IN THE REFRIGERATOR.

EVEN WHEN I'D BEEN INVITED TO A FRIEND'S PARTY, IT WAS THE SAME. HIS RESPONSE NEVER VARIED. HE WOULD SAY, "BY THE TIME YOU FINISH YOUR WORK, THE PARTY WILL HAVE JUST GOTTEN INTO FULL SWING -- YOU'LL ARRIVE WITH PERFECT TIMING!" OF COURSE, I NEVER HAD AN ANSWER TO THAT.

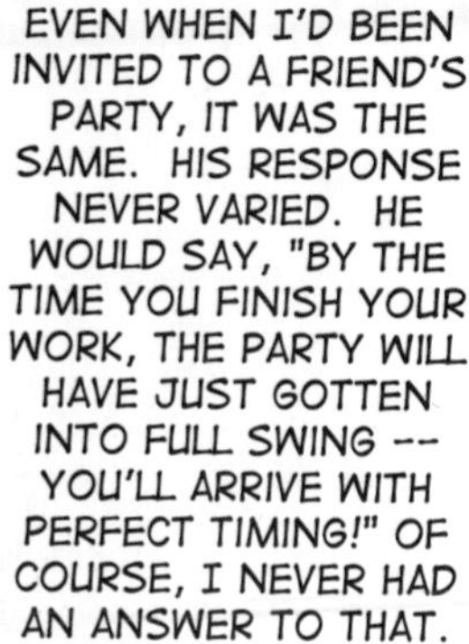

SCRUB
SCRUB
SCRUB
SCRUB...

BY COUNTING TRAYS, I COULD CALCULATE WHEN I WOULD BE FINISHED WORKING, AND THEN I COULD TELL MY FRIENDS WHEN I WOULD BE ARRIVING.

I MUST HAVE BEEN ABOUT SEVEN WHEN I FIRST STOOD IN THE KITCHEN. MY FATHER WAS A VERY STRICT MAN, YOU SEE. IF I EVER WENT OUT TO PLAY BEFORE FINISHING MY WORK AND HE FOUND OUT ABOUT IT, HE WOULD HIT ME HARD ENOUGH TO SEND ME FLYING ACROSS THE ROOM.

OUI, MONSIEUR!!

YOU WERE SUPPOSED TO LAUGH THERE!

I CAME HERE AFTER I GRADUATED COLLEGE IN JAPAN.

WHAT?

22?

BUT THAT MEANS YOU'RE ONLY THREE YEARS YOUNGER THAN I AM! IT'S HARD TO TELL WITH ASIANS ...I THOUGHT YOU WERE STILL IN YOUR TEENS.

A COLLEGE GRADUATE, AND YOU CAME ALL THE WAY TO PARIS JUST SO YOU COULD BE A PEON IN SOME BAKERY? JAPAN IS AN ECONOMIC GIANT -- THERE MUST BE BETTER JOBS YOU COULD FIND THERE!

WHY?

BECAUSE I'M GAY.

WHETHER I KEPT IT HIDDEN OR I OPENED UP TO IT, I THOUGHT IT WOULD BE DIFFICULT IN A CORPORATE ENVIRONMENT.
THE YEAR I GRADUATED FROM COLLEGE, I CAME OUT TO MY PARENTS...AND IT BECAME DIFFICULT FOR ME TO STAY AT HOME, TOO. AT THE TIME, IT JUST SO HAPPENED THAT THE BOY I WAS SEEING SAID HE WAS GOING TO PARIS TO STUDY, AND SO I...I GUESS I JUST WANTED TO BE ANYWHERE BUT JAPAN.
BUT, YOU DON'T EVEN WANT TO BE A PASTRY CHEF, DO YOU? AT THIS RATE, YOU'LL END UP AS A GRUNT YOUR WHOLE LIFE.
YOU'RE RIGHT.
BUT I DON'T MIND.
AS LONG AS I'VE GOT MONEY ENOUGH FOR THAT DAY, AND A MAN WHO WILL SPEND ONE NIGHT WITH ME...THAT'S ALL I NEED.
n-Baptist
Hevens
SMACK!!

AFTER ALL THOSE TIMES I TOLD YOU NOT TO ACT ON YOUR OWN WHEN I'M NOT HERE...
...I'M SORRY, MONSIEUR.
WHY DID YOU DO IT?!
MR. ERIC -- THE CUSTOMER WHO ALWAYS BUYS OUR CROISSANTS -- HE ASKED ME TO. HE SAID IF MONSIEUR HEVENS WASN'T HERE, THEN HE DIDN'T MIND IF I DID IT, SO COULD I BAKE UP A BATCH BEFORE EVENING...I'D HELPED MAKE THE DOUGH BEFORE, AND I KNEW HOW TO DO IT, SO...
THE CROISSANT! THE APPLE PIE! THE CHOCOLATE ECLAIR! THE QUALITY OF THESE THREE ITEMS DETERMINES THE QUALITY OF THE STORE! HOW DARE YOU ACT IN SUCH A WAY AS TO DAMAGE THE REPUTATION OF MY SHOP! NOW HURRY UP AND REMOVE ALL THE CROISSANTS YOU BAKED FROM THE SHELVES!!
...OUI, MON...
DO YOU WANT TO BE HIT AGAIN?!
OUI, MONSIEUR! I'LL GO RIGHT AWAY!
HURRY UP!!

OUI, MONSIEUR!
HOW CAN YOU ANSWER SO HONESTLY? WHY...WITH THAT BALD-HEADED OLD MAN...?
HONEST...
HE WAS ALWAYS SAYING HOW ADORABLE I WAS.
DO YOU SLEEP WITH ANYONE WHO CALLS YOU ADORABLE?!
YOU SLEPT WITH ERIC, DIDN'T YOU...?
OUI, M...
......!
THEN I'LL TELL YOU! I'VE ALWAYS ADORED YOU! EVER SINCE WE FIRST MET!!
AND NOW YOU'RE TELLING ME THAT BALD HEAD HAS BEEN REFLECTED IN YOUR BLACK, DOE-LIKE EYES... AND HIS FAT, CATERPILLAR-LIKE FINGERS HAVE CRAWLED OVER YOUR IVORY FLESH?!
THERE'S NO WAY TO PREDICT THEIR NEXT REACTION...
I...I DON'T GET THE FRENCH...
I JUST ASSUMED THAT YOU HAD A LOVER WAITING FOR YOU BACK IN JAPAN, SO I RESTRAINED MYSELF! BUT YOU...YOU...! WITH ERIC, OF ALL PEOPLE...!

YES, I'M GAY, TOO...
I'M SORRY I HIT YOU...IT WAS HALF OUT OF JEALOUSY.
...I KNEW.
HEY, JEAN-BAPTISTE.
IF I TOLD YOU...THAT ERIC WAS JUST A ONE-NIGHT STAND, AND THAT I'D BROKEN IT OFF WITH MY STUDENT BOYFRIEND LONG AGO...WHAT WOULD YOU DO?
HM?
SHK!
HUH? ISN'T THAT THE CROISSANT THAT I...
......!

IS THIS REALLY THE FIRST TIME YOU'VE MADE THIS?
YES, BUT...?
YUSUKE.
I'M GOING TO TEACH YOU A TRADE. FROM NOW ON, YOU WILL WORK UNDER ME, TRAINING IN THE ART OF PASTRY- AND BREAD-MAKING! THIS IS AN ORDER!
WHAAAT?!
WRONG ANSWER!!
OH, UH...OUI, MONSIEUR.
COLOR IS CRUCIAL FOR A BAKED PASTRY! IF IT'S TOO FLOURY-WHITE OR BURNT-BLACK, IT WILL NOT APPEAL TO THE CUSTOMER! TRY AGAIN!!
NO GOOD!
OUI, MONSIEUR!

THIS IS NO GOOD **EITHER!** UNTIL YOU CAN BAKE THIS IN A BEAUTIFUL GOLDEN COLOR, DON'T COME HOME TONIGHT!
OUI, MONSIEUR!
DON'T ANSWER ME IN THAT SULLEN TONE!
OUI, **MONSIEUR!!**
EEEK... I HATE THIS INTENSE SPORTS-TRAINING FEEL... THIS IS WHY I NEVER JOINED SPORTS TEAMS AT SCHOOL!
OH...! YOUR POOR HANDS HAVE BECOME SO ROUGH...
FORGIVE ME, YUSUKE, FOR RUINING YOUR BEAUTIFUL HANDS...OH, MY YUSUKE...!
...AND I STILL DON'T UNDER-STAND FRENCH-MEN...
THEN BE KIND TO ME DURING THE DAY!
NOT BAD!
IT GOES WITHOUT SAYING THAT THE QUALITY OF THE INGREDIENTS IS IMPORTANT.
THE CREAM AND BUTTER ARE ALL FROM ECHIRE. THE FRUITS ARE ONLY THE CREAM OF THE CROP FROM THE RHONE VALLEY REGION. THE CHOCOLATE IS FROM VERONA, AND THE FISH FOR THE TRAITEUR ARE FRESHLY CAUGHT OFF THE COAST OF BOULOGNE-SUR-MER AND DELIVERED OVERNIGHT.

OUR *APPLE CHIBOUST* NEEDS A SIGNATURE ACCENT THAT REPRESENTS OUR STORE...
THE APPLES ARE VERY GOOD... THEY'VE RETAINED THEIR CRISP TEXTURE, AND ARE BOTH TART AND SWEET.
HMM...THEN WHAT ABOUT FLAVORING THE CREAM WITH APPLE BRANDY? THAT WILL INCREASE BOTH THE AROMA AND FLAVOR, AND GIVE THE CAKE MORE PUNCH.

THIS IS...!

DELICIOUS!!

DELICIOUS!!

DEE-LICIOUS!!

THE CAKE I HAD THE OTHER DAY WAS FABULOUS! THANKS TO YOU, IT WAS A WONDERFUL PARTY. YOUR PASTRIES ARE CERTAINLY THE BEST!
THANK YOU VERY MUCH!
IT'S ASTONISHING! YOUR PASTRIES ARE ALWAYS IMPROVING. I HEAR YOU'LL BE MOVING YOUR STORE TO RUE SAINT-HONOR SOON -- *CONGRATULATIONS!*
CAN YOU TELL ME WHAT YOUR RECOMMENDED CAKE FOR THE DAY IS?

TODAY I RECOMMEND THE *LIME CHIBOUST*.
THE CHIBOUST IS A HOUSE SPECIALTY OF OURS, BUT WE'VE MADE THIS ONE WITH CITRUS FRUIT. THE BOTTOM LAYER CONSISTS OF PINE NUTS AND WALNUTS MIXED WITH CHOCOLATE.
IT'S TART IN FLAVOR, BUT YOU ARE SURE TO ENJOY THE CONTRAST OF THE SMOOTH CHIBOUST, WHICH MELTS IN YOUR MOUTH AS DELICATELY AS VIRGIN SNOW, AND THE CRUNCHY TEXTURE OF THE BASE. IT IS A CAKE AS REFRESHING AS YOUR BEAUTY, MADAM.

OH!

HE'S SO GOOD TO THE CUSTOMERS! THEY'D NEVER SUSPECT THAT HE ONLY EVER YELLS OR HITS AT US!
MONSIEUR HEVENS CERTAINLY HAS BECOME THE PRINCE OF THE INDUSTRY! HE'S HANDSOME TOO, SO I GUESS IT WAS INEVITABLE. BUT REALLY, MR. ONO, THAT LIME CHIBOUST WAS YOUR...
OH NO, ALL I DID WAS COME UP WITH THE IDEA.
ARE ALL JAPANESE PEOPLE SO SELFLESS?
IF I HAD YOUR TALENT, I'D HAVE BRANCHED OFF ON MY OWN LONG AGO.
I'M FINE WITH THE WAY THINGS ARE.
BY THE WAY, JEAN-BAPTISTE SAID HE'S GOT TO GO TO A FRIEND'S PARTY AND HE WON'T BE HOME TONIGHT.

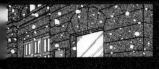

OH GOOD! THEN I'LL BE WAITING AT MY APARTMENT AFTER WORK!
ARE YOU FINDING FAULT WITH HOW I RUN MY BUSINESS?!

I NEVER SAID THAT.
IT'S ONLY NATURAL TO THINK OF EXPANDING THE STORE, AND IT'S TRUE THAT THE BUSINESS OPERATIONS OF A BAKERY MUST BE UNIFIED IF IT IS TO LAST.
BUT...YOU'RE AN ARTIST AT-HEART, AREN'T YOU? I JUST THOUGHT IT WOULD BE EASIER FOR YOU IF YOU LEFT THE HANDLING OF PR AND MANAGEMENT TO A SPECIALIST IN THOSE FIELDS.
OH, I GET IT -- THIS *"SPECIALIST"* IS YOUR NEW LOVER, RIGHT? WHEN DID YOU LEARN HOW TO TALK SO BIG TO ME, EH?!
...I HEAR THAT ALAN VERGNE WANTS TO WELCOME YOU AS A PÂTISSIER AT HIS SHOP.
IT'S A GOOD OFFER! A CAREER OF JUST THREE YEARS AS A PÂTISSIER, AND ALREADY YOU'VE BEEN HEADHUNTED BY A PARISIAN THREE-STAR RESTAURANT! IT'S UNHEARD-OF!
BUT...THAT OFFER... I WAS GOING TO TURN IT DOWN...
WHY? YOU SHOULD GO! I KNOW WHAT EVERYONE IS SAYING-- THAT IT WOULD HAVE TAKEN JEAN-BAPTISTE HEVENS ANOTHER FIVE YEARS TO ESTABLISH A STORE IN A PREMIER LOCATION IN PARIS IF IT WASN'T FOR THAT JAPANESE PÂTISSIER!

OR WHAT?! DID YOU SEDUCE ALAN VERGNE WITH YOUR BODY, TOO -- JUST LIKE YOU SLEPT WITH THAT SNOTTY LITTLE BRUNETTE APPRENTICE?
...NOW PROMISE ME. I'LL STILL FORGIVE YOU IF YOU SAY YOU'LL NEVER SLEEP WITH OTHER MEN AGAIN!
...KNOWING THAT'S A PROMISE I CAN'T KEEP? JEAN-BAPTISTE...
YOU WHORE!!
......G!!

IT'S ALWAYS LIKE THIS...! I HIT YOU, REGRET IT, AND END UP CRAWLING BACK TO YOU ON MY KNEES IN APOLOGY...I'VE HAD ENOUGH!
GET OUT...!!
OK.
I WILL. THANKS FOR EVERYTHING.
I WAS JUST A BUSINESSMAN AFTER ALL.
BUT JEAN-BAPTISTE...
YOU'RE THE ONE THAT BUILT THE STORE UP TO WHERE IT IS...NOT ME. HAVEN'T YOU ALWAYS SAID? SOMEONE WHO CAN ONLY THINK OF PASTRY-MAKING AS A BUSINESS SHOULD NEVER BECOME AN ARTISAN...IF THE DESIRE TO MAKE THE CUSTOMER HAPPY IS NOT IN HIS HEART, HE CAN NEVER MAKE GOOD PASTRIES...
GOOD-BYE.

THUNK
BAM!
CLAK
CREAK
CLICK...

WAIT!

YUSUKE!!

YUSUKE!

WAIT, YUSUKE! I WAS WRONG! I WENT TOO FAR!!

DON'T GO, YUSUKE!

YUSUKE!!

I LOVE YOU...!!
HMM...IT WAS LIKE ONE OF THOSE FRENCH FILMS -- TWO PEOPLE MEET AND HAVE SEX FIFTEEN MINUTES INTO THE MOVIE, AND THEN SPEND THE NEXT HOUR AND FORTY-FIVE MINUTES JUST FIGHTING AND ARGUING...

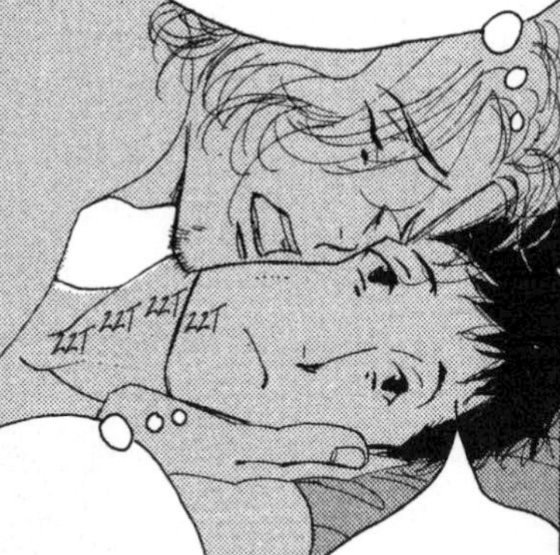
ZZT ZZT ZZT ZZT
HIS STUBBLE HURTS...
I STILL REGRET THAT TIME. I WAS STILL IMMATURE BACK THEN...OH, TO BE ABLE TO HOLD YOU IN MY ARMS AGAIN LIKE THIS! YOU FORGIVE ME -- DON'T YOU, YUSUKE...?

I LOVE YOU...

Fin.

TRANSLATION BY: YUSUKE ONO

THEN WHO ARE YOU SLEEPING WITH NOW?
YOU MEAN TACHIBANA? NEVER! I'VE ***NEVER*** SLEPT WITH HIM. ***REALLY!!***
WHO...? WELL...UM, NO ONE IN PARTICULAR, BUT...
WHAT?!

ME NEITHER! EVEN AFTER WE PARTED, I COULDN'T STOP THINKING ABOUT YOU, AND...!!

......
......
......

ZZT
ZZT
ZZT

.....!!

OH, HOW KIND YOU ARE...!!

FORGIVE YOU...? NO NO, ***JEAN-BAPTISTE!*** I WAS THE ONE IN-THE-WRONG...

HUH?

OW... OW OW OWW!

I KNOW...! YOU'RE TOO KIND. THAT'S WHY YOU CAN'T TURN ANY MAN AWAY! THAT STORE OWNER WHO CAN ONLY SPEAK STILTED TEXTBOOK FRENCH, LIKE AN ANNOUNCER...YOU SLEPT WITH HIM OUT OF KINDNESS TOO, RIGHT?

ZZT
ZZT
ZZT
ZZT
ZZT

AFTERWARDS...
AFTER YOU WERE GONE, I HIT ROCK BOTTOM. MANY OF THE OTHER EMPLOYEES QUIT IN SUCCESSION, TOO...THAT WAS WHEN I FINALLY REALIZED MY METHODS WERE WRONG.
I WENT BACK TO CONCENTRATING ON THE BAKING, AND HIRED AN OUTSIDE SOURCE TO MANAGE BUSINESS OPERATIONS FOR ME, JUST AS YOU SAID. I STOPPED ACTING LIKE A DESPOT IN THE STORE... AND I NO LONGER HIT THE APPRENTI IN FITS OF RAGE.

...BUT ONLY AFTER YOU HAD ALREADY GONE...

WHEN THE HOTEL RITZ SAID THEY WANTED TO OPEN A PATISSERIE SHOP WITH MY NAME ON IT, I WAS READY TO REFUSE. I WAS GOING TO TURN THEM DOWN, WHEN SUDDENLY, I REMEMBERED-- THERE WAS ONE OTHER PERSON IN THIS WORLD, AN ARTISAN, WHO WOULD BE ABLE TO PERFECTLY RECREATE THE TASTE OF MY CREATIONS.

THAT'S *YOU*. TODAY, WHEN I ATE THOSE PASTRIES YOU MADE... I CONFIRMED IT. YOU'RE THE ONLY ONE WHO CAN DO IT.

AFTER THAT, EVERYTHING WENT WELL.

THE STORE BECAME A SUCCESS. BUT SINCE I WANTED TO BE CLOSE ENOUGH TO OVERSEE EVERY ONE OF MY CAKES BEING MADE, I PURPOSELY CHOSE NOT TO OPEN ANY OTHER SHOPS. THIS MADE THE STORE EVEN ***MORE*** POPULAR.

ARE YOU STILL UNABLE TO FIND ANY MEANING IN YOUR WORK BESIDES THE MONEY?
JEA...

THEN YOU SHOULD COME BACK TO PARIS AND WORK FOR ME AGAIN.

...BECAUSE I PROMISE TO PAY YOU THREE TIMES THE MONEY YOU'RE MAKING NOW...WITH NO STRINGS ATTACHED!

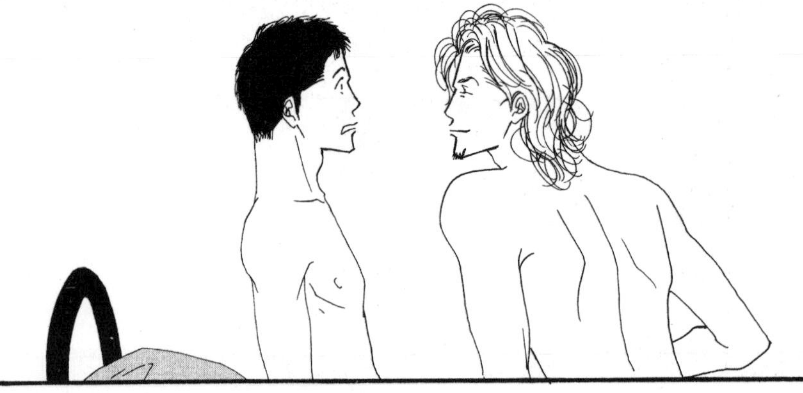

FORGIVE ME...BUT WHEN I HEARD THAT, A SINGLE THOUGHT FLASHED THROUGH MY HEAD:
WITH THAT SALARY, I COULD ALSO BUY A PAIR OF PRADA SANDALS TO GO WITH THE PANTS!

I WAS IN MY SECOND YEAR OF JUNIOR HIGH.

THE TWO PEOPLE IN MY PARENTS' BEDROOM WERE MY MOTHER AND THE TEACHER IN CHARGE OF MY CLASS.

"IF YUSUKE FINDS OUT, THEN HE FINDS OUT. I'LL SHOW YOU HOW GOOD A WOMAN CAN BE, TEACHER..."

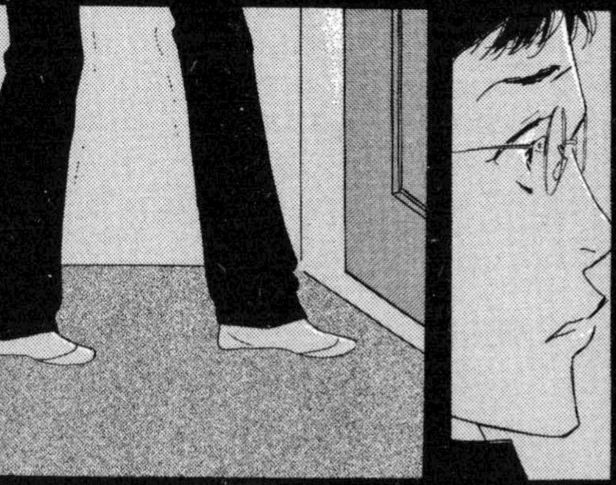

MY MOTHER HAD ALWAYS BEEN RATHER CARELESS... SHE MUST HAVE FORGOTTEN THAT I WOULD BE HOME EARLY FROM THE TUTORING SCHOOL THAT DAY.

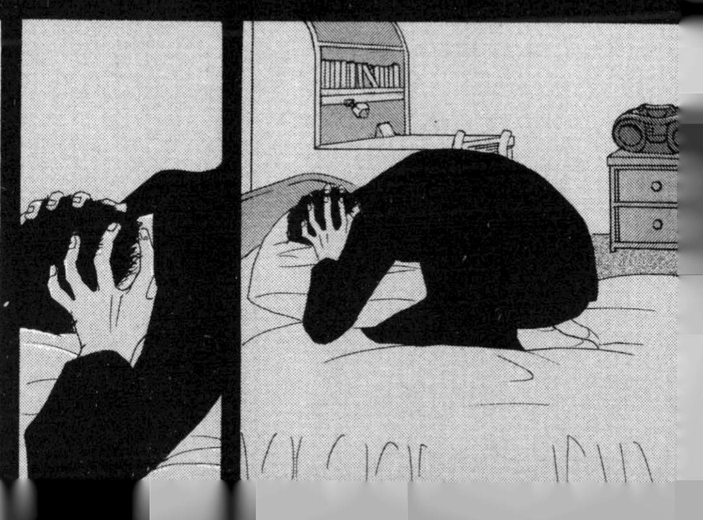

SO AS NOT TO WAKE MY SLEEPING SISTERS, I PLUNGED MY HEAD INTO THE PILLOW AND CRIED. I HATED MY MOTHER.

Recipe 12 (part 2)

CHIRP
CHIRP
CHIRP
N...

…
…
FFH
FFH
FFH
CREAK…
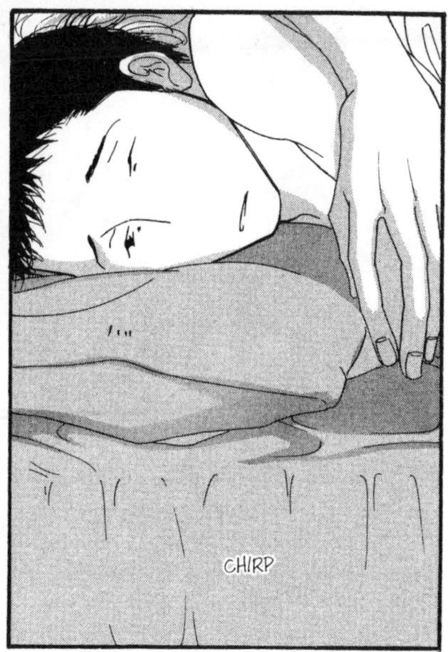
CHIRP

……
……
CHIRP
CHIRP
CHIRP
CHIRP
CRAK
CRAK
KRIK
FFH
FFH
FFH

HEAD-HUNTED ...?!
YEAH.
AND THE OFFER?!

TO BE THE CHEF PÂTISSIER OF A BRANCH OF HIS STORE, AT THE HOTEL RITZ IN PARIS, WITH AN ANNUAL SALARY OF ABOUT 25,000,000 YEN.
リッツすか!!
THE RITZ!!

GEEZER! IT'S ALL YOUR FAULT, GEEZER!! BECAUSE YOU WERE TOO CHEAP ABOUT HIS BONUS!! AND WHAT'S THE RITZ?!
A FIVE-STAR HOTEL IN PARIS! AND THE SALARY I'M GIVING HIM IS STILL A LOT BETTER THAN SOME OF THE OTHER STORES!!
HMMM...

WHAT SHOULD I DO...

B-BUT MASTER! IF YOU LEAVE, I...THERE'S STILL SO MUCH MORE I WANT TO LEARN FROM YOU...!!
WHAT?!
I...I KNOW...
...
...

DDDDDOES THIS MEAN MR. ONO WILL BE QUITTING THIS STORE?! NOOO, MR. ONOOOOO!!
SO SLOW ON THE UPTAKE...
MASTERRR~!!
WAIT-WAIT-WAIT!!

CUT IT OUT, YOU TWO! THIS ISN'T FOR US TO SAY!!

IN THE END, ONO'S GOT TO DECIDE FOR HIMSELF.

SLAM!

...
...

OH...! HELLO, MOM?!
HEY, DO YOU KNOW HOW MUCH I HAVE IN ASSETS IN MY NAME?! YEAH, THE ONES I HAVE DIRECT ACCESS TO! WHAT? NOT MUCH?! BECAUSE GRAMPS IS STILL ALIVE?! I THOUGHT SO...
YOU'LL LEND ME MONEY?! ...NO, NO, THAT'S OKAY... IF I BORROW ANY MORE, I WON'T BE ABLE TO PAY IT BACK...NOT WITH THIS STORE'S ANNUAL PROFITS...

G' NIGHT! GOOD NIGHT... GOOD NIGHT, BYE-BYE.
Antique

DUN!

I KNEW YOU WENT OFF SOMEWHERE AT NOON...BUT THIS IS WHAT YOU WERE OUT BUYING?
IT DOESN'T MATTER, JUST TAKE A BITE OF EACH! PLEASE! OK, EIJI?!

OH, ALL RIGHT THEN...!
BITE!

BITE!

BITE!
BITE! BITE! BITE!

HOW ARE THEY?!
ALL RECOMMENDED CAKES OF FAMOUS BAKERIES! THERE MUST BE ONE IN THERE THAT MAKES YOU THINK THE MAKER IS WORTHY OF BEING YOUR MASTER!!

HMMM... I STILL SAY OUR CAKES MAKE THE BEST LATE-NIGHT SNACKS...

COME ON~! DON'T SAY THAT -- PICK ONE! DO YOU REALLY LIKE THAT GAY GUY'S CAKES SO MUCH?!

HEY, CAN I EAT ONE OF OUR STORE'S CAKES TO GET THE TASTE OF THESE OUT OF MY MOUTH?

JEAN...I ASKED YOU TO WAIT FOR ME AT HOME...
WHAT DOES IT MATTER? I COULDN'T WAIT TO SEE YOU... LET'S GO HOME TOGETHER.

OH...

Antique
ZEEK
ZEEK
ZEEK
Antique
YUSUKE.

MR. ONO...
I'LL NEVER UNDER-STAND...
I WONDER WHY THOSE GUYS CAN'T WALK DOWN THE STREET WITHOUT THEIR HANDS CLAMPED ON EACH OTHERS' BUTTS...?
OH, COME ON! IT'S OBVIOUSLY NOT A MONEY ISSUE...I'M NO GAY, BUT IT'S PRETTY OBVIOUS THEY MUST BE SLEEPING TOGETHER...

HELLO! IT'S **SO** HOT TODAY!

ZEEK
ZEEK
ZEEK
tique

THE MASTER... I WONDER IF HE'S LEAVING...

WELCOME...YES IT HAS BEEN SO HOT LATELY, HASN'T IT...IF YOU ARE DINING IN, OUR SPECIAL TODAY IS A RARE CHEESECAKE WITH A SCOOP OF PEACH ICE CREAM...♡

A-ARE YOU OK? YOU'VE BEEN SO BUSY LATELY. YOU MUST BE TIRED...? TAKEOUT IS FINE WITH ME...
NO, NO...NO WORRIES... PLEASE STAY AND TAKE YOUR TIME...
HAHAHA... BUT I AM SO GLAD THAT IT WAS A KIND CUSTOMER LIKE **YOU** THAT CAME IN HERE TODAY...

DEPRESSING!

I KNEW SHE'D SHOW UP...
COME ON, **HURRY UP!** EXPLAIN THINGS TO ME!
YES...IF YOU ARE BUYING TO TAKE HOME, MAY I RECOMMEND THE POMME VERTE -- A MOUSSE MADE FROM GREEN APPLES. IT IS A CAKE AS COOL AND SHARP AS YOU ARE, MADAM...
THIS MAN...NO MATTER WHAT THE SITUATION...

Antique

ONO.

GOT A MINUTE? I WANT TO TALK TO YOU.

Danny's
Danny's
24

... ...

AH AH AH AH! WAIT, ONO -- DON'T TAKE THIS THE WRONG WAY. IT WOULD ***NEVER EVER EVER EVER*** HAPPEN...IT WOULD NEVER HAPPEN, BUT...
WOULD ANYONE LIKE A REFILL?
UM...

...IF I SAID I'D SLEEP WITH YOU, WOULD YOU STAY AT OUR STORE?!

H...

TURN!

WOULD ANYONE LIKE A REFILL...

HAHAHAHAHA-
HAHAHAHAHA-
HAHA!!
BUMP

I HAD NO INTENTION OF LEAVING, FROM THE BEGINNING.

BESIDES, I DON'T REALLY WANT TO SLEEP WITH YOU ANYMORE, TACHIBANA.
UNLESS YOU REALLY INSIST..
CRACK
SOUND OF INJURED PRIDE!

...THE REASON I'VE BEEN LOOKING SO THOUGHTFUL LATELY IS BECAUSE JEAN-BAPTISTE IS ALREADY ENTHUSIASTIC ABOUT TAKING ME BACK TO PARIS. I'M TRYING TO THINK OF A WAY TO TURN HIM DOWN GENTLY. HE CAN BE A LITTLE UNPREDICTABLE WHEN HE GETS ANGRY.

YOU...!! AND HERE I WAS, REVEALING MYSELF LIKE AN EDO-ERA MAIDEN FORCED TO UNDRESS IN FRONT OF A CORRUPT MAGISTRATE TO SAVE HER FAMILY...!!
OH, YOU WERE? SORRY, SORRY... AND BY THE WAY...

IT'S GOTTEN A BIT MORE COMPLICATED NOW THAT I'VE SLEPT WITH HIM ALREADY... SO I GUESS I'LL HAVE TO BE PREPARED FOR SOME KIND OF TANTRUM, AT LEAST.

SO, YOU HAVEN'T GIVEN HIM ANY ANSWER YET REGARDING THE JOB OFFER?!

HE GAVE ME THE OFFER AFTER WE'D ALREADY HAD SEX, SO I WASN'T REALLY IN ANY POSITION TO SAY, "NON."

YOU WERE SEEING HIM ***AFTER*** THAT, THOUGH!

WELL, BECAUSE WE'VE BEEN SO BUSY AT THE SHOP, I HADN'T HAD ANY ACTION LATELY, SO...YOU KNOW...

BUT HE'S GOT A SHORT FUSE, HASN'T HE?!

HE'S NOT A BAD MAN...

YOU KNOW, IF YOU GO ON LIKE THIS, ONE DAY YOU'RE GOING TO BE STABBED IN THE STREET...
MAYBE...

THE REASON I HATED MY MOTHER BACK THEN WAS NOT BECAUSE SHE WAS BETRAYING OUR KIND FATHER, OR THE FACT THAT SHE WAS HAVING SEX IN THE ROOM RIGHT NEXT TO MY SLEEPING LITTLE SISTERS.

I THOUGHT YOU WERE A LITTLE MORE ADEPT AT HANDLING LIFE, BUT YOU'RE ACTUALLY PRETTY RECKLESS.

I WAS JEALOUS.

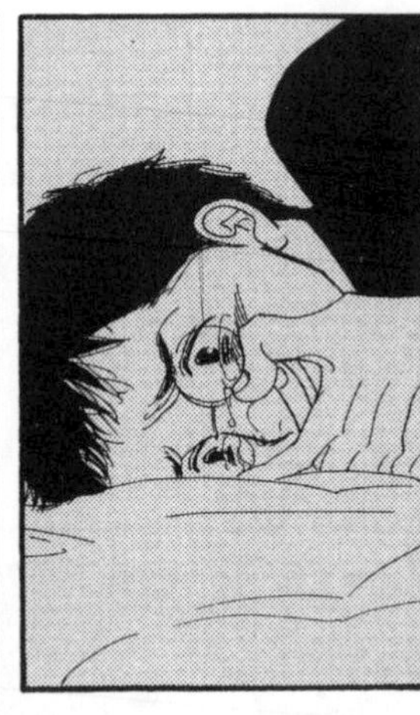

I HATED HER BECAUSE SHE WAS SLEEPING WITH THE FIRST MAN I'D EVER FALLEN IN LOVE WITH.

WOULD ANYONE LIKE A REFILL?

I'VE NEVER REALLY CARED ABOUT BEING GOOD TO MYSELF, SO...

THE FACT THAT I FELT THIS WAY MADE ME THINK THAT I MUST BE EVEN WORSE THAN HER.

BUT IT'S NOT REALLY SOMETHING YOU HAVE ANY CONTROL OVER, YOU KNOW?
OH, I'M SORRY, MY COFFEE'S GOTTEN COLD -- COULD I GET A FRESH CUP?
YES, SIR. RIGHT AWAY...
SOMETHING YOU HAVE CONTROL OVER...
...I GUESS NOT...

CHI.
BED HAIR.

CHIRP
CHIRP
CHIRP

HURRAY! SO MR. ONO IS GOING TO STAY AT OUR STORE FOREVER!!
バンザーイ!!
バンザーイ!!
BANZAAI! BANZAAI!
ACTUALLY, WHEN I HEARD HIM SAY IT, I WANTED TO BANZAI, TOO.
RRRRRR

EIJI?
HUH? NO, I HAVEN'T HEARD ANYTHING FROM ONO.

THERE'S NO ANSWER ON HIS HOME PHONE OR HIS CELL. THE MASTER'S NEVER BEEN LATE TO WORK BEFORE...

BUT HE SHOULD HAVE BEEN HERE AT THE STORE BY NOW.

I'LL CALL YOU BACK LATER. BYE.
MY LORD?!

ANYWAY, YOU KEEP WORKING. WORST CASE SCENARIO, BE PREPARED TO OPEN THE STORE WITHOUT ONO. GOT IT?
OK.
I GOT IT.
YEAH, I'LL TRY GOING OVER TO HIS PLACE.

HAS SOMETHING HAPPENED TO MR. ONO?!
I DON'T KNOW THAT YET. ANYWAY, YOU GET READY AND GO ON AHEAD TO THE STORE. I MIGHT NOT BE ABLE TO GET THERE IN TIME FOR OPENING, BUT...
I'M GOING WITH YOU!

I'M GOING WITH YOU!

I SAID...!
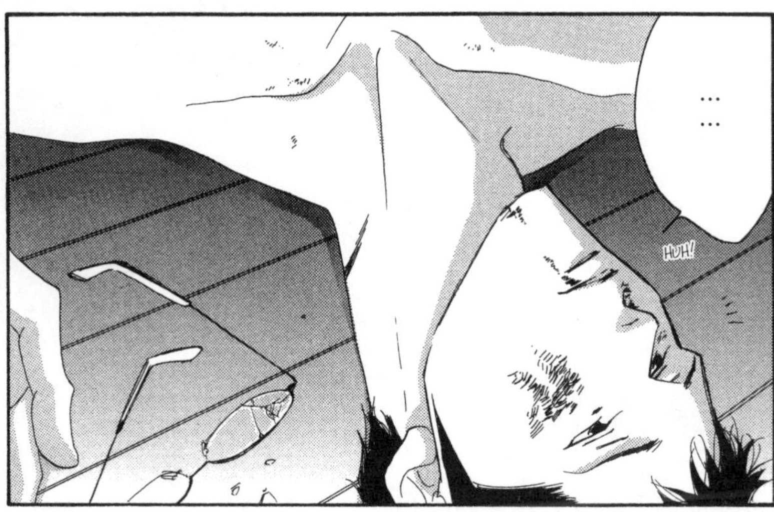
...
...
HUH!

...
TATTERED...
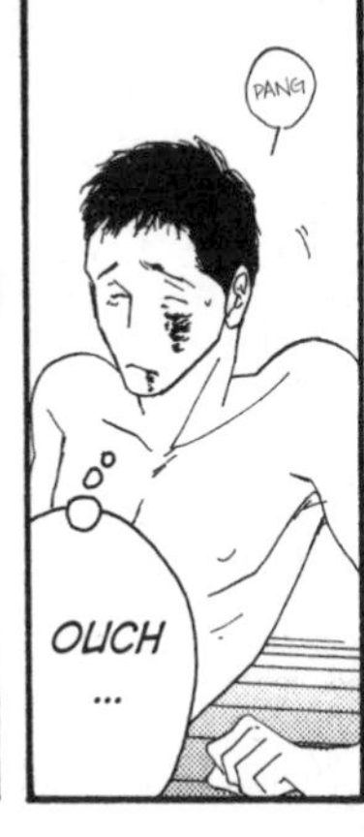
PANG
OUCH
...

CHAK
CHIK
CHAK

SO, YOU WON'T RECONSIDER...

I'M SORRY...
OH...A NOSE-BLEED...
HUH?

WHY?! IT'S THREE TIMES YOUR CURRENT SALARY! IS JAPAN SO KIND TO GAYS?!
AAAH!!

I'M LATE...!

YUSUKE!
HEY, ARE YOU OKAY FOR YOUR GIG AT THE HOTEL?! I'M LATE! I HAVE TO GO.

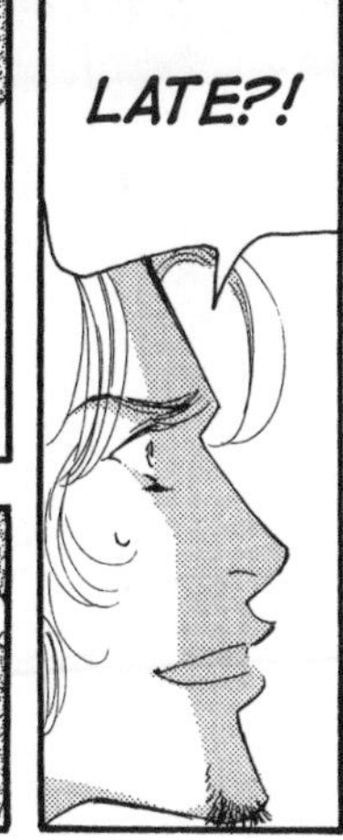

LATE?!

GRAB!

OW...!

WHAT?! LATE?! WHAT REASON DO YOU HAVE TO BE SO DEDICATED? OR TO FOLLOW MY TEACHINGS EXACTLY TO MAKE THE BEST PASTRIES? OR TO RELY ON YOUR EXCEPTIONAL TALENT AND CONJURE UP A DELICIOUS TASTE NO ONE HAS EXPERIENCED BEFORE?
IF YOU HAVE NO NEED FOR THEM, WHY NOT GIVE YOURSELF TO ME. YOUR TALENTS ARE THE VERY THINGS I HAVE BEEN AFTER ALL MY LIFE!!

HEY, YUSUKE... SHALL I DESTROY YOUR RIGHT HAND, HERE AND NOW? TO ME, IT IS A HAND OF GOLD...BUT FOR YOU, IT'S NOTHING BUT AN ORDINARY HAND, RIGHT...?

WHAT?
Y-YOU'RE JOKING...
WAIT...

ピンポーン
DING DONG
!
N...
NO... NOT MY HAND...!!

OH, IT'S OPEN!
CHAK!
HEY, ONO -- YOU HERE?!

OH.

I KNEW IT WOULD BE SOMETHING LIKE THIS...
MR. ONO?!

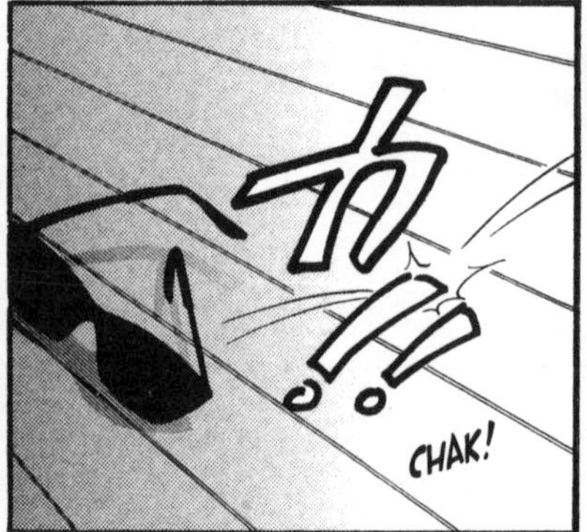
カ!!
CHAK!

ガッ!
GRAB!

U...
UGH!
GET AWAY FROM MR. ONO!
GET AWAY FROM MR. ONO.
MR. CHIKAGE!!

NO! NOT HIS RIGHT HAND! HE'S STILL GOT TO GO TO WORK AFTER THIS! PLEASE, LET HIM GO!!
OWWW OWWW OWWWWW!!
BUT IF I LET GO, HE HITS!
OH, LET HIM GO ALREADY, CHIKAGE...HE WON'T HIT ANYMORE.

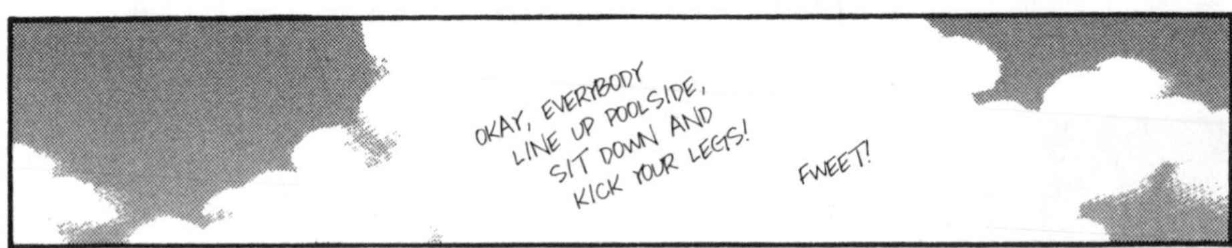
FWEET!
OKAY, EVERYBODY LINE UP POOLSIDE, SIT DOWN AND KICK YOUR LEGS!

OKAY, KICK KICK KICK!
SPLASH SPLASH SPLASH SPLASH
EEEK!
IT'S COLD!

EEEK!
SPLASH SPLASH SPLASH SPLASH
PRRRR

YEAH, IT'S ME.
IT LOOKS LIKE WE'LL MAKE IT FOR STORE-OPENING. ARE YOU OK ON YOUR OWN? I'LL FILL YOU IN ON THE DETAILS WHEN I GET THERE.
YEAH.
YEAH.
BYE.
P!

THAT BLONDE GAVE UP PRETTY EASILY.

THANKS... IT WAS A GOOD THING YOU GUYS SHOWED UP.
WHAT A TROUBLEMAKER! AND CHIKAGE INSISTED ON TAGGING ALONG... WHEN I TOLD HIM TO GO ON HIS OWN THEN, HE SAID I HAD TO COME WITH HIM BECAUSE HE WAS AFRAID OF GETTING LOST!
WHICH IS THE MASTER ..?
HUHH? BUT...
SORRY...

DECIDING YOU DON'T WANT TO DIE IS GOOD, BUT IT'S ALREADY TOO LATE IF IT'S AFTER YOU'VE BEEN STABBED. I'M GONNA GO ON AHEAD TO THE STORE.

OH, YEAH... APOLOGIZE TO KANDA FOR ME.
YOU TWO BETTER GET THERE SOON, TOO!

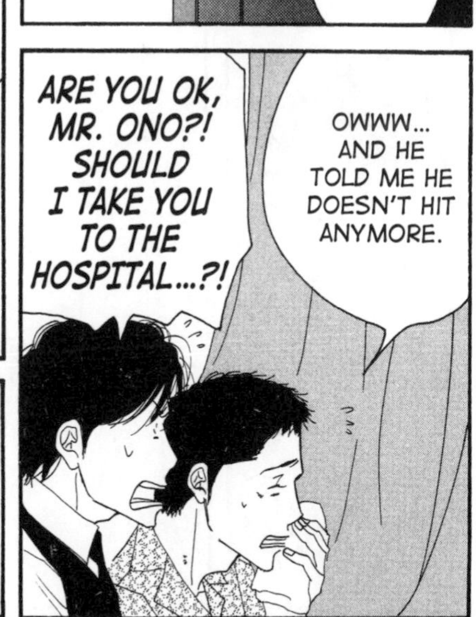
SLAM
OWWW... AND HE TOLD ME HE DOESN'T HIT ANYMORE.
ARE YOU OK, MR. ONO?! SHOULD I TAKE YOU TO THE HOSPITAL...?!

OH, NO... IT'S NOTHING. I'M FINE.
THIS HAS HAPPENED MANY TIMES BEFORE...USUALLY I'M THE ONE AT FAULT. OF COURSE THAT ONE TIME I TOOK ON FIVE GUYS AT ONCE, I GOT A LITTLE WORRIED OF CATCHING SOMETHING AND WENT TO GET CHECKED OUT AT THE HOSPITAL, BUT...

... ...

DRIBBLE

PITTER
PATTER
PITTER

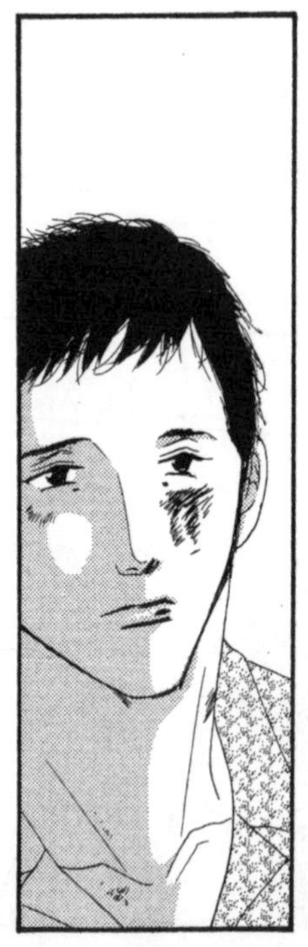

PLEASE DON'T SAY SUCH SAD THINGS...

DRIBBLE DRIBBLE

SIGH...
IT'S THE NATURE OF BEING A MAN... MY BODY IS BATTERED AND BRUISED, BUT SEEING HIM MAKE SUCH A FACE STILL AROUSES ME...

COME TO THINK OF IT...

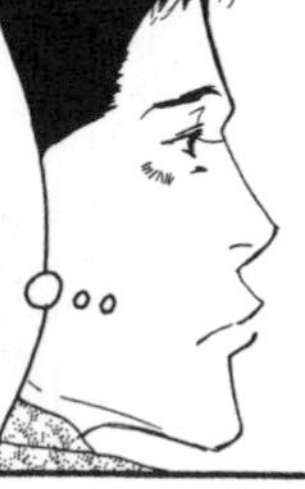
I USED TO CRY A LOT IN THE PAST, TOO. THAT TIME TACHIBANA DUMPED ME, I CRIED MY EYES OUT ON THE TRAIN HOME AND WEIRDED OUT THE OTHER PASSENGERS. ME, A GROWN MALE STUDENT, BAWLING IN PUBLIC. I REALLY LOVED TACHIBANA BACK THEN...AND THAT TEACHER FROM MY CLASS, TOO...

...
...

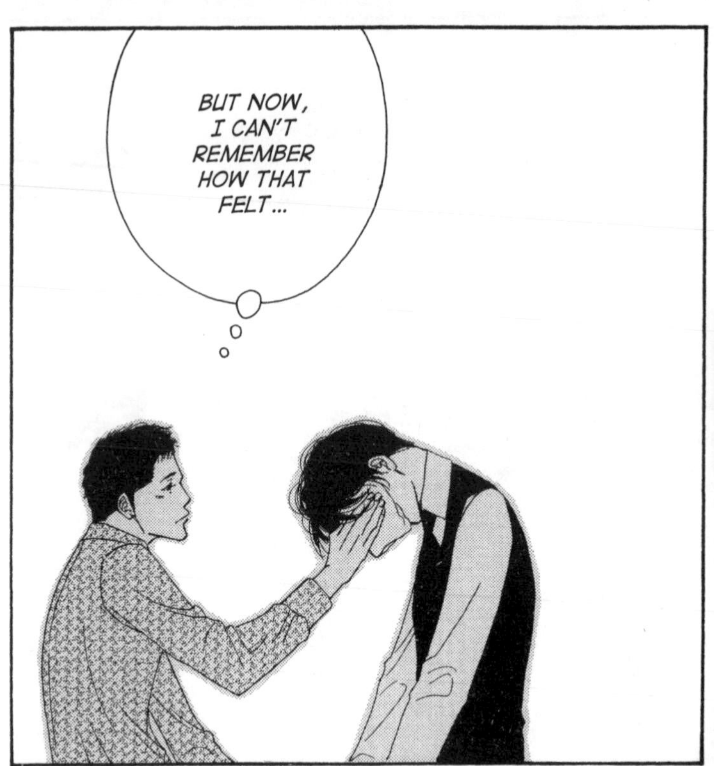
BUT NOW, I CAN'T REMEMBER HOW THAT FELT...

Antique
ZEEK ZEEK
COO COO
ZEEK

...SO, LONG STORY SHORT, ONO'S A LITTLE HURT FROM HIS SCUFFLE WITH THE BLONDE, BUT DON'T YOU GO OFF ON A REVENGE SPREE WHEN YOU SEE HIM LIKE THAT!
HEY, I'M A FORMER PRO BOXER! HOW COULD I HIT AN AMATEUR?

SORRY I'M LATE...

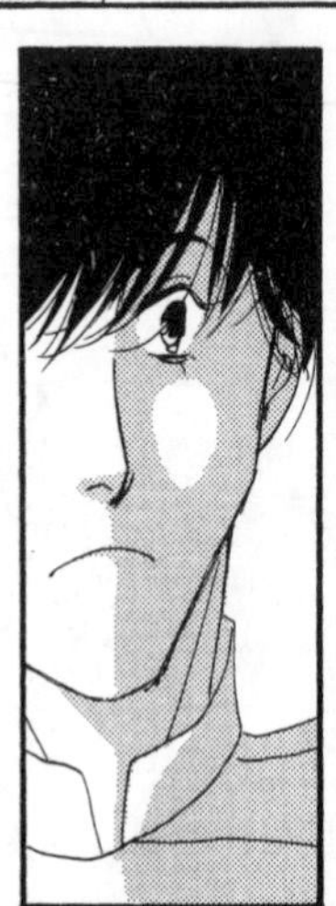

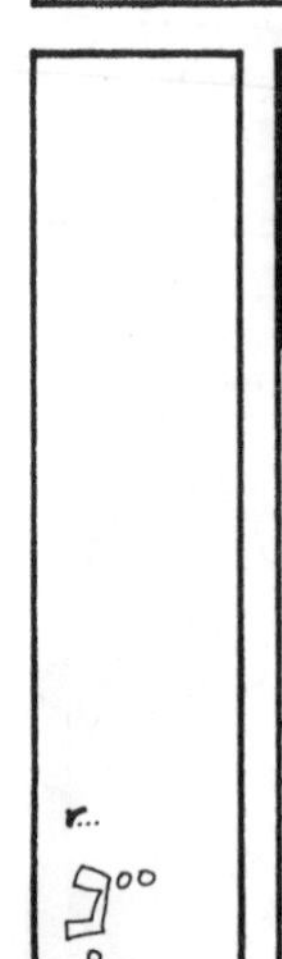
r...

THAT FOREIGNER, HOW DARE HE HIT THE MASTER...!!
OH, DON'T WORRY, AFTER ALL YOU'RE THE MASTER'S TEACHER -- I'LL JUST SLAM YOU A BODY BLOW WITH THIS GOLDEN RIGHT HAND OF MINE AND LET YOU OFF EASY BY LEAVING YOU TO THRASH IN YOUR OWN VOMIT - NOW WHICH HOTEL DID YOU SAY HE'S AT?
THAT'S NOT "FORMER PRO BOXER"... THAT'S JUST "FORMER THUG"!!
RRROOOAAARR
HE'S AT THE HOTEL MOKURA. DO YOU WANT TO GO, KANDA?

WHAT? REALLY, MASTER?!
LET'S GO TOGETHER ON OUR NEXT DAY OFF. MY TREAT, SO YOU CAN EAT AS MANY OF HIS CAKES AS YOU WANT.
HEY, ONO...?!

IT'S A RARE CHANCE TO TASTE THE FINEST AUTHENTIC FRENCH PASTRIES. IT'LL BE A GOOD LEARNING EXPERIENCE FOR YOU. ONCE YOU'VE EATEN HIS CAKES, I DOUBT YOU'LL FEEL LIKE HITTING HIM.

YUSUKE.

I'VE ALWAYS BEEN...

...JEALOUS OF YOUR TALENT.

......

I'M SORRY...

TO TELL YOU THE TRUTH, THERE WAS NEVER A TIME WHEN I THOUGHT WORKING AS A PÂTISSIER WAS FUN. THE ONLY REASON I PUT ENERGY INTO MY WORK WAS BECAUSE, AS A GAY MAN, I KNEW I DIDN'T HAVE A LOT OF JOB OPTIONS.

BUT NOW...

THERE'S THIS BOY AT THE STORE -- MY APPRENTICE. HE'S GOT A GOOD SENSE OF THINGS, AND ABOVE ALL, HE LOVES PASTRIES. WHEN I SAW HIM, I THOUGHT, "HE'S SURE TO BE A GREAT PÂTISSIER SOME DAY."

AND UNTIL I'VE GIVEN HIM ALL THE KNOWLEDGE I POSSESS ABOUT THE ART OF PASTRY-MAKING, I CAN'T LEAVE THIS STORE...

I WANT TO MAKE HIM INTO A FINE ARTISAN... LIKE YOU.

ドキッ
FLINCH

...
...
TAKE CARE...

HMM...I WAS NEVER ABLE TO PREDICT HIS REACTIONS, RIGHT UP UNTIL THE VERY END.
HUH?
OH, THAT'S RIGHT. WE'LL HAVE TO START THINKING UP SOME NEW CAKES FOR THE AUTUMN SEASON, SO YOU COME UP WITH A COUPLE OF TRIAL ITEMS, TOO. OKAY, KANDA?

REALLY? ON MY OWN... FROM SCRATCH?
OF COURSE. BUT IT'S QUITE HARD, YOU KNOW. OUT OF EVERY TEN THAT YOU THINK

I'LL DO MY BEST!

HEY
HEY HEY
YOU GUYS!
ESPECIALLY
YOU, ONO!
臨時賞与
SPECIAL BONUS
BOW
DOWN
BEFORE
ME!

YAAAY~!
THANK YOU
THANK YOU!
TACHIBANA,
I LOVE
YOU!
OH LOOK AT
YOU, YOU'RE
SULKING!
I TOLD YOU
I'D MAKE
YOU MY NEW
MAN IF YOU
REALLY
INSISTED...!
プラダ~
PRADA-!!
!!
HEY, I SAID
BOW DOWN
BEFORE ME!
BESIDES, I'M
JUST A MAN IN
YOUR PAST
NOW, AREN'T I!
HEY,
GEEZER...

I REALLY DON'T NEED THIS MONEY. COULD YOU GIVE MINE TO THE MASTER?

K...KANDA... SO TEMPTING... BUT I COULDN'T TAKE IT.
HEY, THIS MONEY WAS SUPPOSED TO BE FOR SOME NEW SEATS FOR MY FERRARI, YOU KNOW! YOU COULD BE A LITTLE MORE THANKFUL EVEN IF YOU'RE ALREADY ROLLING IN DOUGH FROM BEING A FORMER WORLD CHAMPION BOXER AND ALL.
HUH? I'M NOT ROLLING IN MONEY! I DONATED ALL MY WINNINGS FROM BOXING TO THE INSTITUTE FOR THE HANDICAPPED.

WHAT A BEAUTIFUL SOUL...I'M NOT EVEN WORTHY TO LIE AT HIS FEET...
?
DAMN! AND I WAS GONNA MAKE HIM PUT UP SOME MONEY WHEN WE BUILD OUR SECOND STORE...

WHEN HE THREATENED TO BREAK MY HAND, I ADMIT I GOT A LITTLE FRIGHTENED.

SO FOR THE TIME BEING, I GUESS I'LL TRY NOT TO "GET STABBED IN THE STREET"...ALTHOUGH AT THIS POINT, I DON'T KNOW IF IT WILL DO ANY GOOD.
IT MIGHT. A LITTLE.

WELL, THAT'S THE SITUATION.
NO, I DIDN'T...

DIDN'T YOU REALIZE? THE OTHER DAY AT THE FAMILY RESTAURANT... YOU WERE CASUALLY TALKING TO THE WAITRESS.

HMM?

THANK YOU, TACHIBANA! I'LL REALLY TRY! I WON'T HAVE AFFAIRS! AND WHEN MY SEXUAL URGES BECOME TOO MUCH, I'LL LIMIT IT TO A ONE-NIGHT ORGY WITH NO LINGERING EFFECTS!!
THANK YOU!

HOTEL MŌKURA

WWWWHAT SHOULD I DO...I ALREADY USED UP MY BONUS FOR THE PRADA...I WONDER IF I COULD ASK TACHIBANA TO WRITE THIS OFF LATER AS EXPENSES...
I WONDER...
LADY, BRING ME THIS "PEACH MELBA" THINGY NEXT!

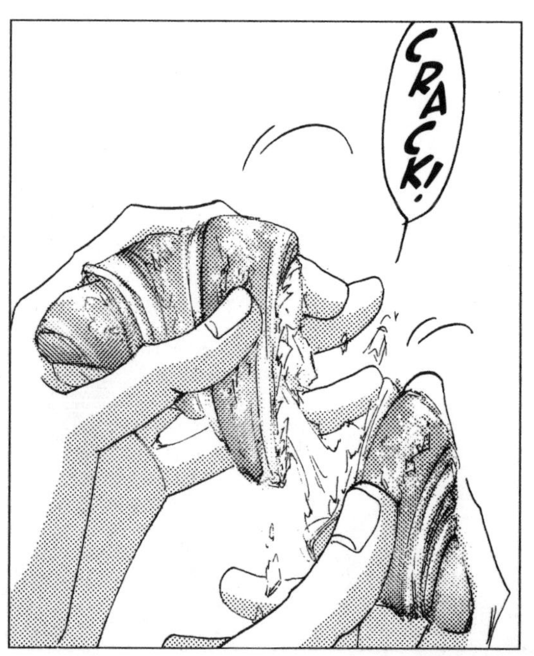
CRACK!

SO...SHE'S REALLY GETTING MARRIED.

I GUESS WE SHOULD GET GOING.

...
...
...
...

SIGH

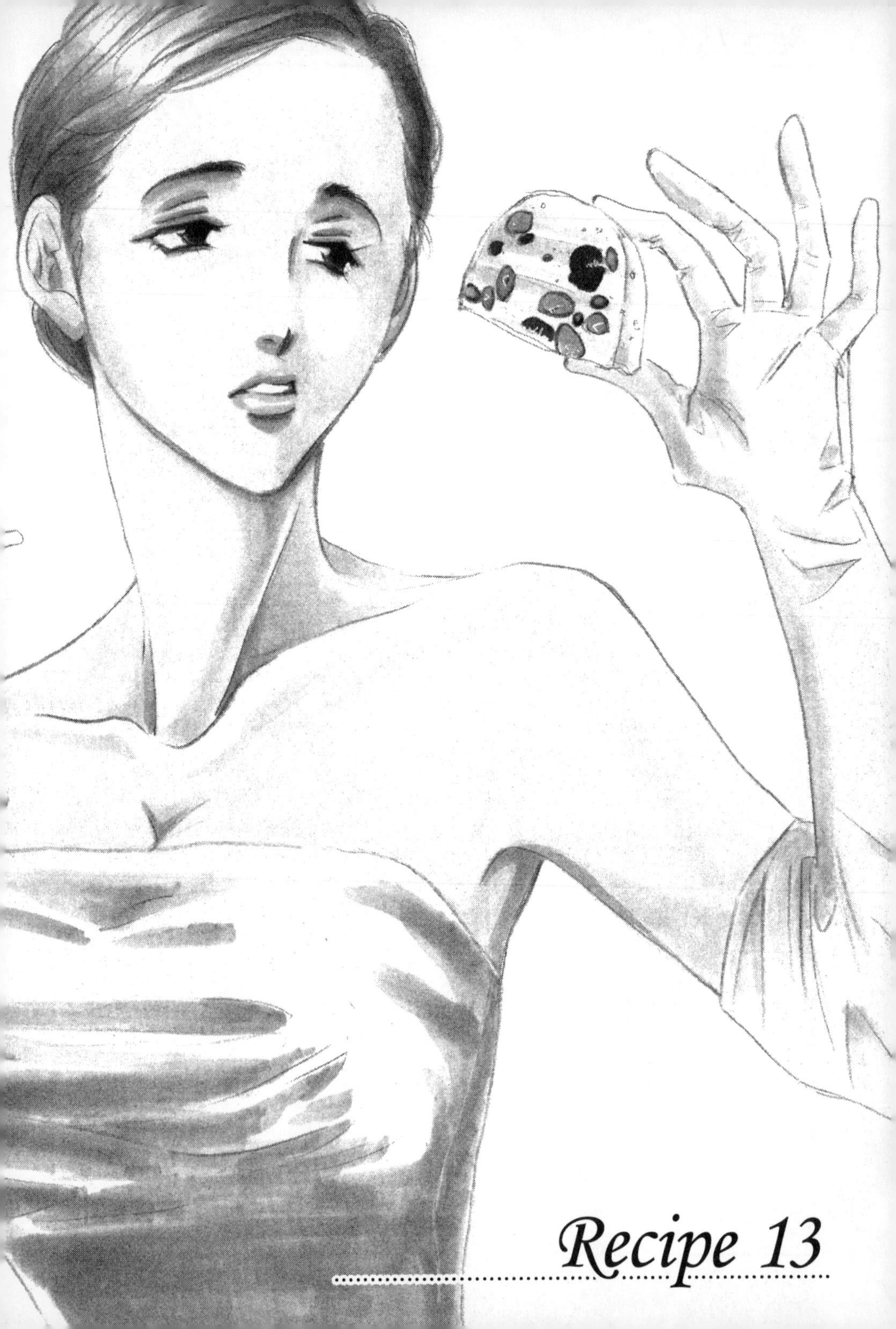

Recipe 13

CONGRA-TULATIONS!

CONGRATULATIONS, MR. KANICHI. SHE'S A BEAUTIFUL BRIDE.

YOU LOOK BEAUTIFUL, TAMIKO. THAT DRESS SUITS YOU.

BUT KAGAMI... WHY IS YOUR DRESS OLIVE-GREEN? AND WHY IS ONLY YOUR HUBBY'S TUXEDO WHITE?
HUUH? BUT I LIKE OLIVE GREEN... AND KAN-CHAN LOOKS BETTER IN WHITE ...
NO MATTER HOW MANY TIMES I LOOK AT HIM, HE STILL LOOKS SO "MINIMALIST"...
YES... AND AS FOR ME...

...I WANT TO DYE MYSELF IN THE COLOR THAT IS MY TAMMY...
SEE?
HE'S MAIDENLY...? A MAIDENLY PUBLIC OFFICIAL...?!

HEY, ISN'T KAGAMI'S HUBBY A PUBLIC OFFICIAL? SO WHERE ARE ALL HIS FRIENDS AND CO-WORKERS?! IN THIS RECESSION, A PUBLIC SERVANT FOR A HUSBAND IS GOLD...GOLD!
THAT'S RIGHT. HE IS A PUBLIC OFFICIAL...AT A DAY-CARE NURSERY. SO HIS CO-WORKERS ARE...LOOK.

ISN'T THAT RIGHT, DIRECTOR?
EXACTLY.
HOHO HOHO!
......

THEY'RE ALL WOMEN!!
THAT'S WHY WE MADE THIS A GARDEN PARTY FEATURING DESSERTS!
DON'T YOU THINK I'M DISAPPOINTED, TOO?!
MS. NAKATSU, I THINK IT'S TIME WE BRING OUT THE WEDDING CAKE SOON.
I'M SAD, TOO... OH TAMMY, I'M A MILLION TIMES BETTER-LOOKING THAN THAT GUY...

OH, HOW PRETTY!

THIS SIMPLE WEDDING CAKE, DECORATED ONLY WITH WHITE ROSES AND GOLD CONFECTION BEADS, IS PERFECT FOR SYMBOLIZING THE START OF A NEW LIFE FOR THIS YOUNG (URK!) COUPLE! SANDWICHED BETWEEN LAYERS OF ***ALMOND-FLAVORED SPONGE CAKE*** ARE A CREAM FULL OF FRESH ***MUSCAT GRAPES*** AND A RICH ***CHOCOLATE MOUSSE***, WHICH HAVE THEN BEEN COVERED WITH A WHIP-CREAM-AND-WHITE-CHOCOLATE FROSTING. TRULY, THIS IS A CAKE FILLED WITH THE TASTE OF AUTUMN! AND NOW, THE NEW BRIDE AND GROOM WILL CUT THE CAKE, SHARING WITH US ALL THIS TRUE TASTE OF HAPPINESS!

I'M A PRO. I WON'T BE OUTDONE BY OLD STUBBLY-MAN.

CLAP CLAP CLAP ETC.

CLAP CLAP CLAP ETC.

パチパチパチ
CLAP CLAP
パチパチ
CLAP ETC.

FOOF!

THIS CAKE IS REALLY GOOD, MRS. TACHIBANA.

OF COURSE! SHE HAD TO MAKE IT...IT'S HER PRIDE AS A CULINARY RESEARCHER.

AT MY HOUSE, OUR CAKES AND EVEN SIDE DISHES ARE STORE-BOUGHT.

WHY THANK YOU, HONMA-KUN. EAT AS MUCH AS YOU LIKE!

YOU'RE LUCKY. EVEN YOUR BIRTHDAY CAKE IS HOMEMADE BY YOUR MOM!

OH? KEIICHIRO, HAVE YOU ALREADY HAD ENOUGH CAKE?

UH...
YEAH. I'M JUST GOING TO THE BATHROOM.
OK.

BUT TO TELL YOU THE TRUTH, SHE USUALLY DOESN'T MAKE CAKES. SHE HAD A HARD TIME! SHE WAS STARING IN THE OVEN THE WHOLE TIME, LIKE, "OH WHAT SHALL I DO IF THE SPONGE CAKE DOESN'T RISE?"
K...KEIICHIRO! YOU PROMISED NOT TO TALK ABOUT THAT!
RRGH!
IT'S ALWAYS LIKE A COMEDY ROUTINE AT THIS FAMILY'S HOUSE.

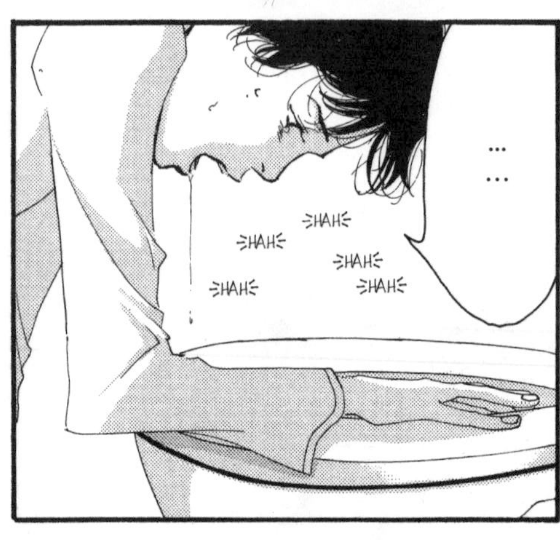
...
...
HAH
HAH
HAH
HAH
HAH

UGH!
COUGH COUGH
COUGH COUGH
URK...

FLOOSH!
I'M SO GLAD MASTER KEI HAS RECOVERED.
THUNK!

AN INTELLIGENT BOY LIKE HIM STILL NOT ABLE TO REMEMBER ANYTHING ABOUT THE ORDEAL...WHEN I THINK ABOUT HOW SCARED THAT CHILD MUST HAVE BEEN, I CAN'T...!

I WONDER...
THAT CHILD...IT HASN'T EVEN BEEN A MONTH SINCE THE INCIDENT, AND HE TELLS ME HE WANTS TO HAVE A BIRTHDAY PARTY...
OH, BUT HE'S EXACTLY THE WAY HE WAS BEFORE! WHY, JUST TODAY HE TOLD THIS VERY FUNNY STORY...IT HAD BOTH ME AND CHIKAGE ROLLING ON THE FLOOR LAUGHING!
HE'S TOO CHEERFUL... HE'S TRYING TOO HARD.

MA'AM
WHAT IF... WHAT IF SOMETHING UNSPEAKABLE WAS DONE TO HIM? IF THAT'S TRUE, THEN...!
KEIICHIRO HAS A WHOLE LONG LIFE AHEAD OF HIM!
WILL HE HAVE TO CARRY THIS SCAR FOR THE REST OF HIS LIFE?! WHAT DID HE DO TO DESERVE THIS...?!

......
I'LL NEVER FORGIVE THE MAN WHO DID THIS!

MMM...!!
OOOH~ I THINK THIS IS THE MOST DELICIOUS WEDDING CAKE I'VE EVER EATEN! THE CHOCOLATE JUST MELTS IN YOUR MOUTH...

THE CAKE IS ***SOOO*** GOOD! THE CHOCOLATE MOUSSE IS SO DELICIOUS...
THANK YOU. IN ORDER TO MAKE THE CHOCOLATE MELT MORE SMOOTHLY, I DIDN'T USE ANY GELATIN IN THE RECIPE...

HEY. DON'T TELL ME YOU'RE OK WITH WOMEN NOW, TOO.
NO WAY. I'M JUST ABLE TO TALK WITH THEM A LITTLE BIT NOW. THAT'S ALL.
I SEE...

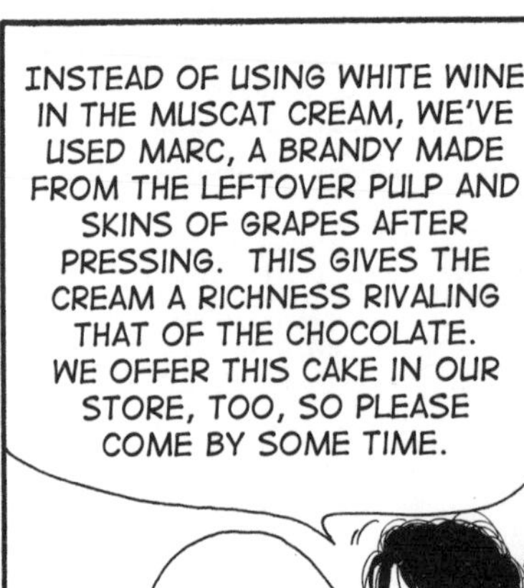
INSTEAD OF USING WHITE WINE IN THE MUSCAT CREAM, WE'VE USED MARC, A BRANDY MADE FROM THE LEFTOVER PULP AND SKINS OF GRAPES AFTER PRESSING. THIS GIVES THE CREAM A RICHNESS RIVALING THAT OF THE CHOCOLATE. WE OFFER THIS CAKE IN OUR STORE, TOO, SO PLEASE COME BY SOME TIME.
WOW... YES, I'LL ***DEFINITELY*** STOP BY!

IN THIS CROWD OF MOSTLY WOMEN, THOSE MEN FROM THE BAKERY REALLY STAND OUT...

UH-HUH...

WHILE HE STAYS A "GAY OF DEMONIC CHARM," THINGS ARE STILL OK...IT'S WHEN HE BECOMES A ***"BI OF DEMONIC CHARM"*** *THAT I'LL* ***FIRE*** *HIM, NO MATTER HOW MUCH THE STORE MAY SUFFER!*

OH MISS NAKATSU, HOW HAVE YOU BEEN?
LONG-TIME, NO-SEE.

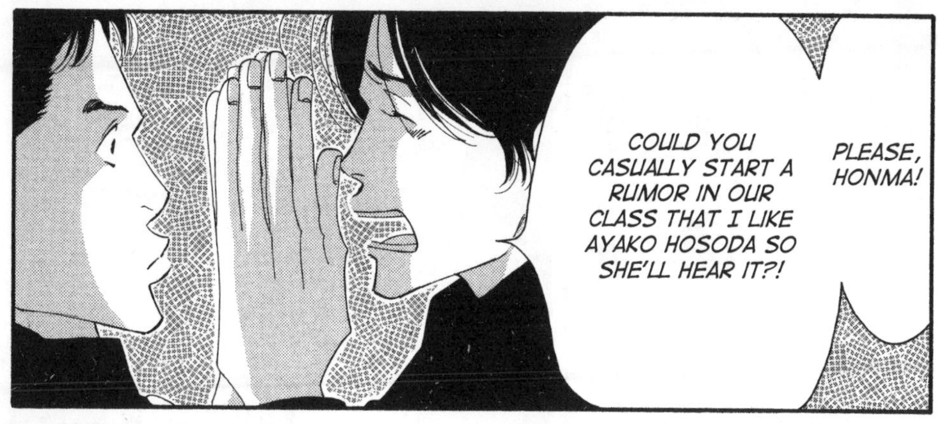
PLEASE, HONMA!
COULD YOU CASUALLY START A RUMOR IN OUR CLASS THAT I LIKE AYAKO HOSODA SO SHE'LL HEAR IT?!

WHAT FOR?
IF HOSODA HEARS ABOUT IT AND SHOWS A FAVORABLE REACTION, I'LL ASK HER OUT!
OH MAN, TACHIBANA-- YOU'VE GOT NO BALLS AT ALL!

HEY, EVEN THE MOST STUDLY OF MEN BECOME WEAK-KNEED AND TIMID IN FRONT OF THEIR TRUE LOVE! GET IT? **GET IT?!**
WHATEVER... I'LL ASK MY GIRLFRIEND ABOUT IT FOR YOU. SHE'S GOT THE SAME CLUB ACTIVITIES AS HOSODA.

REALLY?! OH MAN, THANKS, HONMA! I **REALLY** OWE YOU!
BUT ISN'T HOSODA THAT REALLY TALL, PLAIN-LOOKING GIRL WITH GLASSES? WHY HER? YOU COULD PROBABLY GET SOMEONE MUCH CUTER...

'CUZ SHE'S GOT BIG BREASTS...
HIM AND HIS BIG-BREAST FETISH...

WHAT?! WHAT ARE YOU TALKING ABOUT, SHE'S CUTE! HOSODA IS CUTE!
HOW DO YOU FIGURE?

S...
SURE... I'LL GO OUT WITH YOU.

LISTEN, LISTEN! THEN AFTER THAT, WHEN I GOT HOME, I CALLED HER AT HER HOUSE AND WE TALKED FOR THREE HOURS! IT WAS ALL TRIVIAL STUFF BUT WE TOTALLY CLICKED!
HEY, HONMA -- WHY DO YOU THINK IT IS? HE'S SMART, HE'S GOT THE TOP GRADES IN OUR CLASS, HE SHOWS UP TO SCHOOL IN A CHAUFFER-DRIVEN BENZ EVERY MORNING...BUT SOMEHOW, IT'S IMPOSSIBLE TO HATE HIM.
PROBABLY BECAUSE EVERYTHING HE DOES IS SO CLOWNISH... YOU THINK?

I SEE...SO, YOU DON'T NEED TO BE DRIVEN TO AND FROM SCHOOL? OF COURSE...YOU'RE NOT A LITTLE CHILD ANYMORE.
LITTLE? **NO WAY!** I'M 5'9 NOW! AND I'VE GOT RANKS IN BOTH KENDO AND JUDO.
YOU REALLY DON'T HAVE TO WORRY ABOUT ME ANYMORE, MOTHER.

HEY, HAPPY BIRTHDAY!
OH... JESSYE NORMAN TICKETS! HOW DID YOU...
YOU MENTIONED YOU LIKED SATIE LAST TIME, SO...
THANK YOU...!

HOW'S IT GOIN' WITH HOSODA?

OH...
...WITH AYAKO?

"AYA KO"?

...
...

YOU DID HER! YOU DID IT WITH HOSODA, DIDN'T YOU?!
HEH.
HE HE HE HE... AND A **TREAT** IT WAS.

HUH?

I WANT TO BREAK UP.

WHAT ...?
WH...
WHY ...? AYAKO... WHY ALL OF A SUDDEN...
IT'S NOT SUDDEN.
I'D DECIDED LONG BEFORE. I WAS GOING TO BREAK UP WITH YOU WHEN WE GRADUATED.

WHY?!
OUR COLLEGES ARE IN THE SAME CITY...SO WHY?! DID I DO SOMETHING WRONG?!
YES, YOU DID.
YOU'RE ALWAYS TRYING TOO HARD TO PLEASE ME.

EVERYWHERE I WANT TO GO, EVERY-THING I LIKE TO DO, EVERYTHING I WANT TO BUY!!
WHY GO THROUGH SO MUCH TROUBLE FOR SOMEONE LIKE ME?!

THEY WERE SAYING THAT IF GLASSES ARE YOUR THING, THEN ONO WAS CUTER THAN I WAS...THEY WONDERED WHY YOU WERE GOING OUT WITH SUCH A NOTHING LIKE ME.
THAT'S WHY I GOT CONTACTS... AND CHANGED MY HAIR. BUT I **CAN'T** TAKE IT ANYMORE...!

WHAT ARE YOU TALKING ABOUT? IT'S BECAUSE I LOVE YOU! IT'S BECAUSE I REALLY LIKE TO SEE YOU HAPPY, THAT'S ALL...
YOU SEE? IT'S HARD TO BELIEVE YOU WHEN SUCH SMOOTH WORDS COME SO EASILY FROM YOUR MOUTH.
DO YOU KNOW WHAT EVERYONE WAS SAYING WHEN WE WERE GOING OUT TOGETHER?

WHO SAID THOSE THINGS? JUST TELL ME AND I'LL KICK THEIR...
WHAT DOES IT MATTER? WE'RE GRADUATING TODAY.
AND ANYWAY, YOU LOOK MUCH MORE RELAXED WHEN YOU'RE WITH HONMA AND YOUR FRIENDS THAN WITH ME!

HOW CAN SOME GUY TAKE YOUR PLACE?!
I'M SEEING SOMEONE ELSE.

HE'S NOT AS HANDSOME AS YOU, AND TO BE HONEST, HE'S NO GOOD AT SEX.

BUT I FEEL MORE WANTED WHEN I'M WITH HIM.

DING
DONG
RING
GONG

RING
DING
GONG
DONG

...
...
CLICK

U...
UM...
TACHIBANA, DO YOU HAVE A MINUTE? THERE'S SOMETHING I WANT TO TALK TO YOU ABOUT...

WHAT?

WE'VE FINISHED HANDING OUT THE WEDDING CAKE, SO YOU CAN GO AHEAD AND TRADE PLACES WITH EIJI NOW.
OH, OK... IF YOU SAY SO.
WAS THE VICTIM OF VERY BAD TIMING.

IT'S NICE, ISN'T IT...THE FLOWERS, THE DISHWARE-THE TABLE SETTING IS ALL IN WHITE. IT SETS OFF THE FOOD SO WELL. I'M GOING TO TAKE SOME POINTERS FROM THIS... *SO PROFESSIONAL!*
I'M TOLD THE SPOONS AND FORKS ARE ALL ANTIQUES! THE FACT THAT EACH ONE IS DIFFERENT IS REALLY UNIQUE.

SPEAKING OF WHICH...WHICH FLORIST DID YOU GET THE FLOWERS FROM, TACHIBANA? THEY'RE PRETTY, BUT THEY LOOK EXPENSIVE...
OH, THOSE. I JUST TOOK A CLASS ON FLOWER ARRANGEMENT AND MADE THEM MYSELF. IT WAS EASIER THAT WAY.
HERE YOU ARE...THIS IS A CARAMEL-FLAVORED CHOCOLATE-AND-MARRONS BRULÉE...

THEN WHAT ABOUT THE BRIDAL BOUQUET?!
I MADE IT. WITH SCABIOSAS, LILACS, AND DIAMOND LILIES.
I MADE THE GROOM'S TOO... UNWILLINGLY.
WHAT?!

... ...
I'VE NEVER BEEN THAT IMPRESSED WITH TACHIBANA BEFORE, BUT HE IS REALLY...
YES, AND OVER HERE WE HAVE THE CHEESE-AND-NUTS TARTE.

TADADADADA DADADA~
I MISS YOU IF I WERE ALLOWED I WOULD KEEP ON HOLDING YOU THROUGH THE AFTERNOON LIGHT AND THE STARRY NIGHT...

NO WAY! THIS IS THE FIRST TIME I'VE EVER HEARD "MISSING" SUNG SO WELL! KEIICHIRO, SING "SHOOTING STAR SADDLE" NEXT!
WOOOW!
SURE! I'LL SING ANY REQUEST FROM THE LADY I ADORE, MISS SAEKI.
AND ON TOP OF THAT, HE'S THE ONLY THIRD-YEAR STUDENT OUT OF OUR SEMINAR TO PASS THE DIPLOMATIC SERVICE EXAMINATION.
UNBELIEVABLE... BACK AT THE POOL BAR HE HANDLES THE CUE LIKE A PRO. NOW HE SINGS KUBOTA PERFECTLY...
MONSTER...

SORRY TO SOUND LIKE SUCH A FAN-GIRL, BUT DID YOU SEE "TOKYO LOVE STORY" LAST NIGHT? I LIKE THAT SHOW!
I WATCH IT, TOO. IT'S THAT ONE, RIGHT? THE ONE WHERE RIKA AKANA SAYS TO KANCHI --
"KA~NCHI!"

EVEN IF I'M DRIVEN AWAY BY THE WIND THAT BLOWS TOMORROW...
WHEN SHALL WE SLIP OUT?
RIGHT AFTER I SING "WHERE IS THE SMILE."

......

"LET'S HAVE SEX!"

WHAT? NO WAY!
YOU'VE ALWAYS WANTED TO GO OUT WITH ME...? OH...YOU DON'T HAVE TO TRY SO HARD TO IMPRESS ME, YOU KNOW. BESIDES, YOU KNOW ALREADY, DON'T YOU? I'M GETTING MARRIED AFTER I GRADUATE.
HER EYEBROWS LOOK NORMAL BECAUSE HER MAKEUP CAME OFF...

HUH?!
OH, COME ON...I KNOW YOU'RE A PLAYER! YOUR TECHNIQUE IN BED JUST NOW WAS AS GOOD AS THE RUMORS SAID!
ANYWAY, LET'S REMAIN GOOD SEMPAI-KOHAI FRIENDS OF THE SEMINAR... AND HAVE SEX ONCE IN AWHILE, TOO.

HONMA!!
I WAS IN LOVE WITH HER EVER SINCE I MET HER AT THE SEMINAR!
WHY DOES EVERYONE THINK I'M SUCH A PLAYER? ALL I DID WAS LEARN A LITTLE MORE THAN OTHERS THROUGH CAREFUL RESEARCH OF ADULT VIDEOS AND HOW-TO BOOKS...!!
MAN...SO YOU'RE ABLE TO EXCEL EVEN AT STUFF LIKE THAT, HUH...

I'M NOT GOING TO BECOME A DIPLOMAT. I'M GONNA TAKE THE BAR EXAM INSTEAD.

HUH?!
SHE SAID HER FIANCÉ PASSED THE DIPLOMATIC SERVICE EXAM THIS YEAR, TOO! I DON'T WANT TO SEE HIS FACE!!

WHAT? FOR SUCH A PETTY REASON?! I'M TAKING THE BAR EXAM, TOO -- IF YOU TAKE IT, THAT MEANS ONE LESS OPENING FOR SURE!
NO PROBLEM THERE...'CUZ I'LL DEFINITELY PASS BY NEXT YEAR, BUT YOU'LL NEED ABOUT TWO MORE YEARS OF STUDYING...
...
...

OH?

IT'S DELICIOUS! I'D LOVE TO TAKE SOME OF THIS HOME WITH ME!

I THOUGHT THIS WAS APPLE PIE, BUT THERE'S PUMPKIN INSIDE! WHAT A SURPRISE!
THE "NORMANDE."
UNDER THE SLICES OF CRISPLY-CARAMELIZED RED APPLES LIES A PUMPKIN PASTE FULL OF BUTTER AND CREAM. IT IS A PIE FILLED WITH THE CONTRASTING TARTNESS OF THE APPLE AND SWEETNESS OF THE PUMPKIN.
...

I DID IT! MY FIRST PASTRY IDEA!!
UM...I'M NOT REALLY INTO SWEETS. DO YOU HAVE ANYTHING ELSE...?
HOW SHOULD I KNOW? THEN DON'T EAT!

PARDON ME! HOW ABOUT THIS SEAFOOD COCKTAIL, MADE FROM LAYERS OF COD ROE, SALMON ROE, SCALLOPS AND GELEÉ OF CONSOMMÉ? WE ALSO HAVE MUSSELS SAUTÉED IN GARLIC BUTTER, AS WELL AS A YOUNG CHICKEN STEWED IN OLIVES.
DAMN IT, STUPID EIJI...

OOOH... THIS MUSHROOM QUICHE IS SOOO GOOOD...!!
OK! AFTER WE'VE REFRESHED OUR PALATES WITH THIS, LET'S GO FOR A SECOND ROUND OF CAKES!
huff huff huff
AND WHY IS IT THAT WOMEN HAVE SUCH BOTTOMLESS APPETITES ...?

OOH, NOW I WANNA HAVE SOME.
BUT SAKI, WEREN'T YOU JUST EATING A SWEET BEAN BUN?
I DON'T WANT A WHOLE SERVING, I JUST WANT A TASTE.

ANOTHER TASTE!!
...AND IT'S NEVER JUST A TASTE, EITHER...
BUT KEI'S EGG-FRIED RICE IS REALLY GOOD ♡

ALL RIGHT, THEN... SAY AHHH.
AHHH ...
THERE'S RICE ALL OVER YOUR MOUTH!

HUH?

I'M SORRY...
I CAN'T LIVE WITH YOU, KEI...

...!!
CLANK-!
I WAS HAPPY THAT EVEN AFTER I TOLD YOU ABOUT MY PAST, YOU STILL ASKED ME TO LIVE WITH YOU WHEN WE BOTH PASSED THE BAR EXAM... BUT I'M SORRY.

A...A MAN?!
IS IT ANOTHER MAN?!
UH-UH.
THEN WHY?! WHY?!

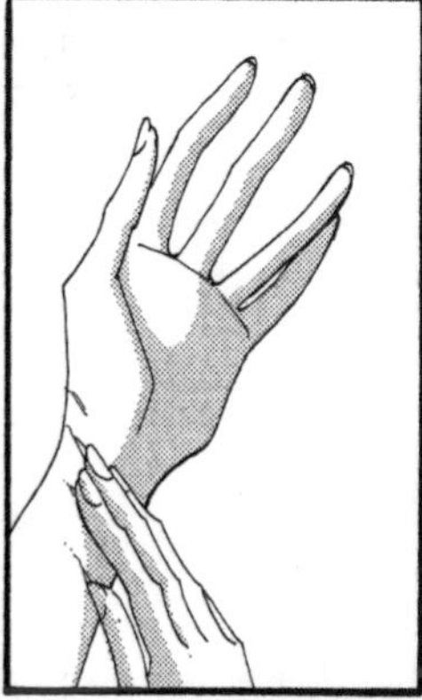

I ALWAYS THOUGHT OF YOU AS A NICE LITTLE SPOILED BOY, HAPPY AND WITHOUT A CARE IN THE WORLD...AND I ALWAYS THOUGHT THAT'S WHAT DREW ME TO YOU.
I THOUGHT SOMEONE LIKE THAT WOULD HELP ERASE THE NEGATIVE SIDE OF ME...

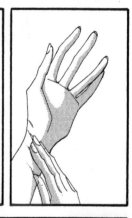

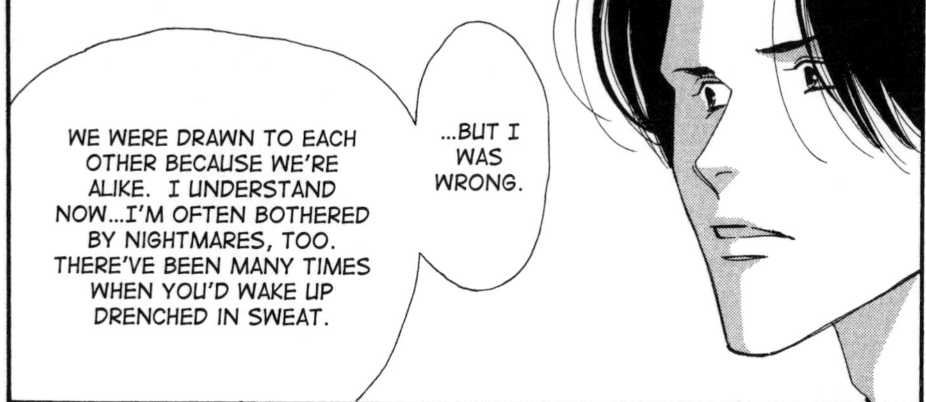
...BUT I WAS WRONG.
WE WERE DRAWN TO EACH OTHER BECAUSE WE'RE ALIKE. I UNDERSTAND NOW...I'M OFTEN BOTHERED BY NIGHTMARES, TOO. THERE'VE BEEN MANY TIMES WHEN YOU'D WAKE UP DRENCHED IN SWEAT.

I'M SORRY YOU HAD TO FORCE YOURSELF TO PUT ON A BRAVE FACE AROUND ME... BUT IT'S OK, YOU DON'T HAVE TO ANYMORE.
IT'S OK...
IT HURTS ME TO SEE YOU TRY SO HARD...

"YOU'RE TRYING TOO HARD."

"HE'S TRYING TOO HARD."

DID YOU EVEN ENJOY OUR SEX...?

I'D ONLY EVER SLEPT WITH AWFUL MEN BEFORE, SO WHEN YOU WERE SO DILIGENT IN BED, IT MADE ME FEEL INSECURE... I OFTEN WONDERED IF I WAS ADEQUATE ENOUGH FOR YOU...
THUD!

HONMA~! I PASSED THE BAR BUT I DON'T WANNA BE A LAWYER ANYMORE! I'M GOING TO LOOK FOR A JOB!
NOT AGAIN!

SAKIKO WAS SMALL-CHESTED, SO I THOUGHT IT WAS TRUE LOVE THIS TIME...BUT FORGET IT...I DON'T WANT TO HAVE TO SEE HER AT THE LAW AND POLICY STUDIES CENTER.
YOU'RE SAYING THIS IN FRONT OF A PERSON WHO ALREADY FAILED IN THE SHORT-ANSWER PORTION OF THE TEST.
BUT IT'S AUTUMN, AND YOU'RE IN YOUR FOURTH YEAR...IT'S GONNA BE HARD TO FIND A JOB AT THIS LATE DATE.

IT'S OK... I CAN GET INTO ONE OF OUR FAMILY'S COMPANIES... I'LL SETTLE FOR THAT.
"SETTLE..."? THAT'S A PLENTY GOOD JOB RIGHT THERE!

I'M HOME...HEY, CHIKAGE - WHAT DOES SEX MEAN TO YOU?
HUH?
CHIKAGE (STILL A COLLEGE STUDENT)

IT'S LIKE A FIELD OF FLOWERS...!

OK! I'LL HELP OUT TOO, MR. CHIKAGE.
10 YEARS LATER, STILL PRETTY MUCH THE SAME PERSON.
SCRUB SCRUB
SCRUB
SCRUB

FORGET IT... FORGET I EVEN ASKED YOU...
?

TEE HEE!

HUH?! B-BUT...!
IT'S OK. TACHIBANA TOLD ME TO WORK BACK HERE.

AUNT, UNCLE...
TAMIKO.
THANK YOU FOR EVERYTHING THESE TEN YEARS.

I PROMISE THAT TAMIKO AND I WILL MAKE A HAPPY FAMILY TOGETHER.

TAMMY ...
THIS IS THE FIRST TIME I'VE SEEN YOU SMILE...

WHAT A GREAT SCENE...
ISN'T IT, THOUGH...?

TYPICALLY, IT WOULD BE PERFECTLY PLAUSIBLE TO FALL IN LOVE IN THIS SITUATION-- BUT NOT WITH THIS ONE.
WE'RE JUST NOT...
...EACH OTHER'S TYPE...

NAKAI FAMILY
ODA FAMILY
WEDDING RECEPTION HALL
中井家
小田家
両家結婚披露宴会場

OH!

?!

...
...

???

MISS MURA-MATSU.
YOU ONLY WRITE ON THE RIGHT SIDE OF THE GUEST BOOK. THAT'S THE BACK OF THE PAPER, AND YOU DON'T WRITE ON THAT SIDE.
WHAT?! REALLY?! I DIDN'T KNOW!

THANK YOU FOR THAT TIME, MR. TACHIBANA... I'M ALWAYS SO SLOW AND CLUMSY. EVEN THOUGH WE'RE RANKED EQUALLY AS CO-WORKERS, I STILL CAN'T CARRY OUT MY WORK A HUNDREDTH AS WELL AS YOU DO.
FINALLY...

I'M NO GOOD AT, THIS, EITHER..
AND THANK YOU FOR HELPING ME THIS TIME, TOO. THEY ASKED ME TO GET THE TEA, BUT...
POUR POUR
IT'S OK...I WAS JUST THINKING ABOUT MAKING SOME FOR MYSELF ANYWAY. THEY REALLY SHOULDN'T BE ASKING SOMEONE IN YOUR POSITION TO DO THINGS LIKE MAKE COPIES OR FETCH TEA...
IT'S JUST MY FAULT FOR NOT BEING ABLE TO SAY NO.

NO, I CAN UNDERSTAND WHY YOU WOULDN'T BE ABLE TO REFUSE.

IT'S ONE THING TO OFFEND A SUPERIOR, BUT IT'S NOT A GOOD IDEA TO UPSET THE GIRLS IN THE GENERAL OFFICE STAFF EITHER. IF I WERE IN YOUR POSITION, I'D BE AFRAID TO REFUSE, TOO.
NOW GO ON -- TAKE THESE BEFORE SOMEONE SEES.

HUH? TAKAGI SEMINAR? THAT'S THE SAME SEMINAR AS HONMA!
HONMA? OH, I REMEMBER HIM! WOW, THAT TAKES ME BACK!

THIS IS IT! WE'VE BEEN GOING OUT FOR A YEAR AND TWO MONTHS, AND WE'RE BOTH 31 YEARS OLD...I BOUGHT THIS RING LEGIT WITH THREE MONTHS OF MY OWN SALARY...AND A WOMAN AT 31 SHOULD BE AT A CRUCIAL STAGE FOR MARRIAGE. THIS TIME IT WILL DEFINITELY WORK! NOW IT'S JUST A QUESTION OF WHEN... WHEN TO GIVE HER THIS...

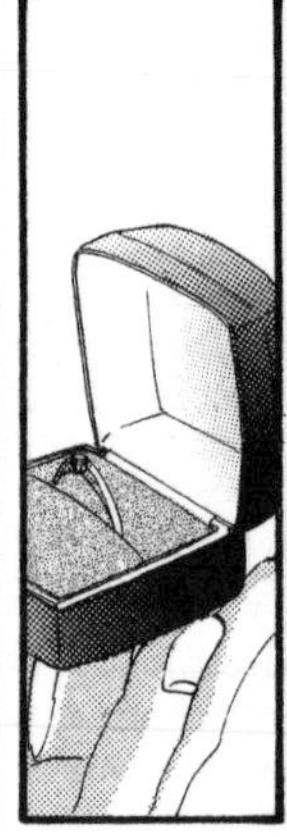

DO YOU HAVE ANY IDEA HOW MUCH YOU'VE COST THIS COMPANY? FOUR-HUNDRED MILLION.
THEY'VE CAN-CELLED.

WHAT...?

WHY DON'T YOU JUST QUIT?! A STUPID WOMAN LIKE YOU, WHOSE ONLY QUALIFICATION IS THAT YOU GRADUATED FROM TODAI...THE ONLY REASON WE KEEP YOU HERE IS FOR APPEARANCE'S SAKE... TO SHOW HOW EQUAL-OPPORTUNITY WE ARE! AND THIS IS HOW YOU REPAY US?!
I'M VERY SORRY! I'LL CONTACT THE OTHER PARTY RIGHT AWAY, AND...!!
I'M SO SORRY!
DON'T BOTHER APOLOGIZING! I'M ASKING YOU TO HURRY UP AND QUIT!!
I AM VERY SORRY!
...UGH!
NOW...
IT'S NOW!!
YEAH!

KEII CHIRO...
SHH... COME ON NOW...YOU DON'T HAVE TO GET SO WORKED UP ABOUT IT.
SOB
SOB
SOB
SOB
HIC
HIC
WHAT SHOULD I DO...
WHAT SHOULD I DO...

IF IT'S REALLY THAT HARD FOR YOU, YOU SHOULD JUST QUIT.
IF IT COMES DOWN TO IT, I'LL TAKE CARE OF YOU FOR THE REST OF YOUR LIFE...OK?

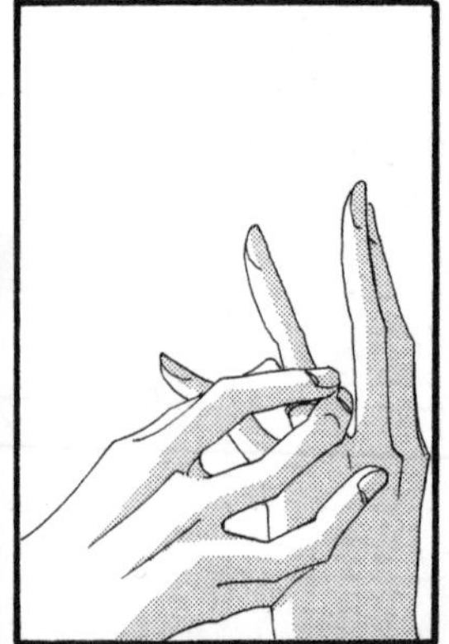

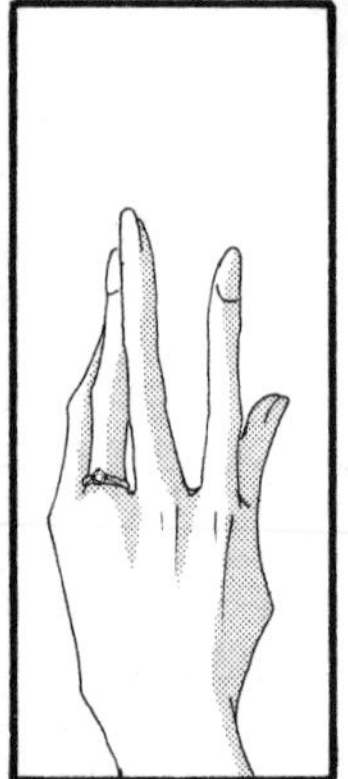

SO, YOU THOUGHT ALL WOMEN WOULD JUST FALL FOR A LINE LIKE THAT...

I DON'T WANT TO QUIT HERE! EVEN IF NO ONE ELSE WOULD SAY IT, I THOUGHT YOU WOULD TELL ME TO KEEP TRYING!

I THOUGHT YOU WERE THE ONLY ONE WHO CONSIDERED ME AS AN EQUAL AT WORK...!

LEAVE.
PLEASE LEAVE. I CAN'T ACCEPT THIS RING.
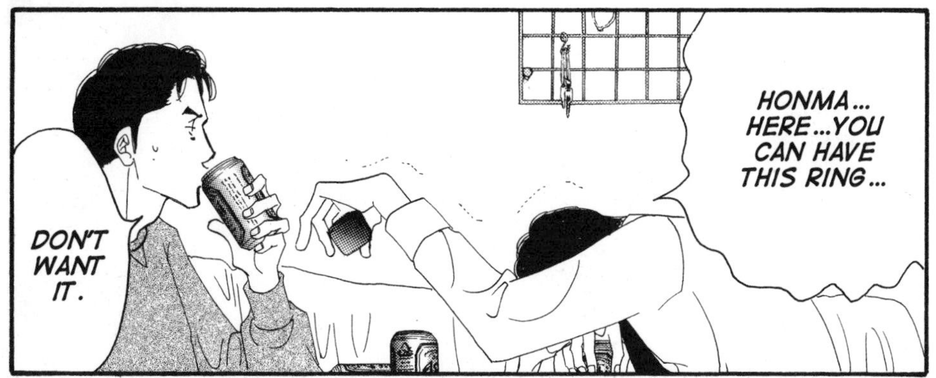
HONMA... HERE...YOU CAN HAVE THIS RING...
DON'T WANT IT.

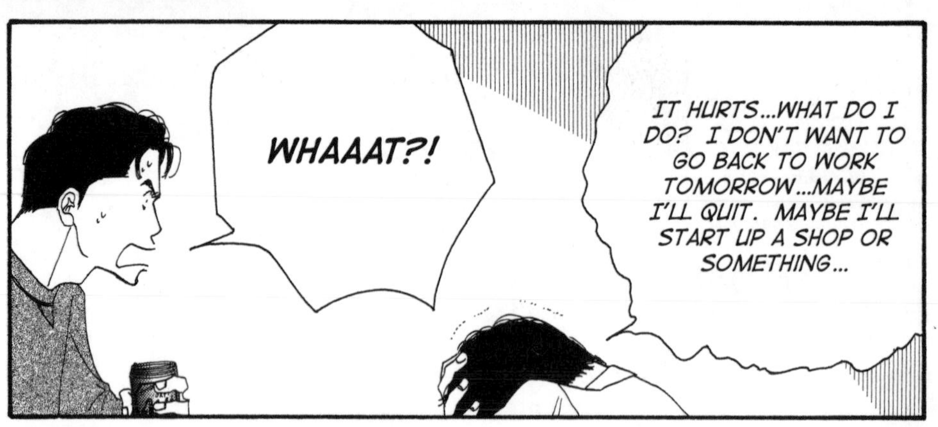
IT HURTS...WHAT DO I DO? I DON'T WANT TO GO BACK TO WORK TOMORROW...MAYBE I'LL QUIT. MAYBE I'LL START UP A SHOP OR SOMETHING...
WHAAAT?!

DO YOU THINK THAT MEANS MOLESTING ME WAS HIS GOAL? DO YOU THINK THAT'S WHY I CAN'T REMEMBER ANYTHING THAT HAPPENED? DO YOU THINK AN EXPERIENCE LIKE THAT WARPS A PERSON SOMEHOW?
UNTIL THE GUY IS CAUGHT OR I GET MY MEMORY BACK... I WONDER... IS MY WHOLE LIFE GONNA BE LIKE THIS...?

YOU'RE IN THE SAME DEPARTMENT THAT SHE IS -- JUST GO BACK AND EXPLAIN TO HER...APOLOGIZE! WHY DO YOU ALWAYS JUST...
H-HOLD ON, TACHIBANA!
HEY, HONMA... WHEN I WAS KIDNAPPED, THE ABDUCTOR NEVER ONCE ASKED FOR A RANSOM OF ANY KIND.

HEY, HONMA... DID YOU GAIN WEIGHT?
HUH?
TACHI-BANA...
YOU...
ALL THIS TIME, THAT'S WHAT YOU'VE BEEN...

AAAGH!!
YOU SEE, THIS IS HOW MEN DESCEND INTO MIDDLE AGE! UGH, HOW HORRIBLE! I'M GONNA BE MORE CAREFUL!
...
...
I'M SENSITIVE ABOUT IT, TOO, YOU KNOW...

...
...
A SHOP... THERE'S ONLY ONE KIND IT CAN BE...
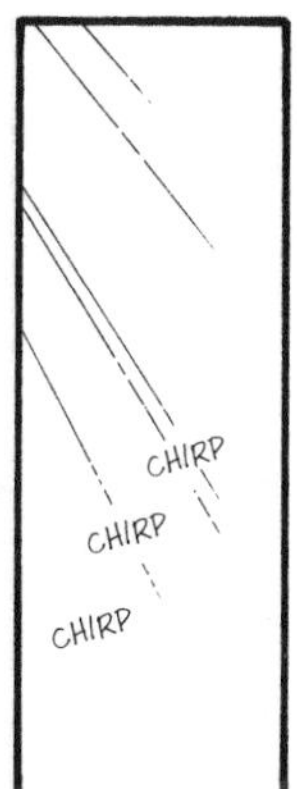
CHIRP
CHIRP
CHIRP

UGH... I FEEL SICK... I DON'T WANNA GO IN TO WORK...
CHIRP
CHIRP
CHIRP

Antique

CHIRP

HUH?

THIS STORE IS NOW OUT OF BUSINESS. WE APOLOGIZE FOR ANY INCONVENIENCE.
-OWNER, MASUOKA ANTIQUES
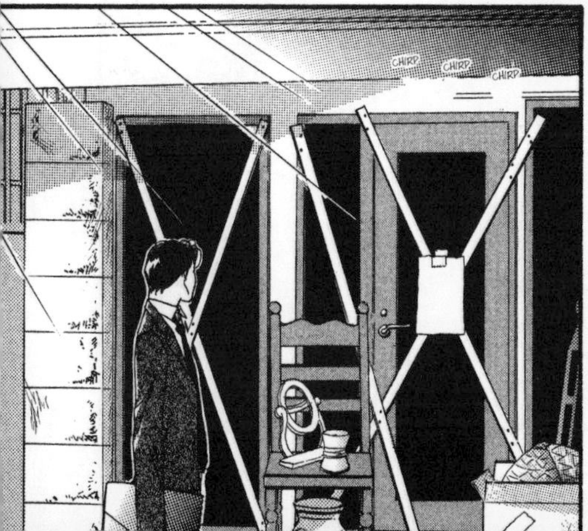
CHIRP
CHIRP
CHIRP

チューウしろ!
KISS HER!
チューウしろー!
KISS HER!
チューウしろ!!
kiss her!

わあーっ!!
YAAAAY!
SMOOCH
ヒュー
FWEE
ヒュー
FWEE
ヒュー
FWEE
パチパチ
CLAP
パチパチ
CLAP

SO LUCKY ...

Recipe 14

NEXT WEEK I'LL BE SHOWING YOU HOW TO MAKE FRIED EGGPLANTS WITH GINGER, CRAB-AND-GINGER STEAMED RICE, AND SASHIMI SALAD USING WHITE FISH.

THANK YOU FOR YOUR LESSON TODAY, MRS. TACHIBANA.

I'M GOING TO TRY MAKING THE OCTOPUS-AND-PLUM RICE YOU TAUGHT US TO MAKE TODAY FOR DINNER. YOUR RECIPES ARE ALWAYS SO HELPFUL FOR ENTERTAINING.

I'M SO GLAD, MRS. ICHINOSEKI. IT'S A VERY EASY DISH, ISN'T IT? AND IT TASTES GOOD COLD AS WELL, SO IT'S VERY HANDY TO MAKE AHEAD OF TIME.

GOOD-BYE, MRS. FUJITANI! SEE YOU AGAIN NEXT WEEK.

WAIT,
MRS. SHINJO! MRS. CHIZUKO SHINJO!

OH...

BRAZIL COFFEE

IT'S YOUR HUSBAND AGAIN, ISN'T IT? MRS. SHINJO!

....

IT'S SO EMBARRASSING... BUT IT'S NOT AS BAD AS BEFORE. SINCE I'VE BEEN TAKING YOUR CLASSES, THERE ARE DAYS WHEN HE GLADLY EATS MY COOKING...
WHAT ARE YOU SAYING?!
I SAW UNDER YOUR SLEEVE. I KNOW ABOUT YOUR COUNTLESS BRUISES. IT'S GETTING WORSE AND ***WORSE!!***
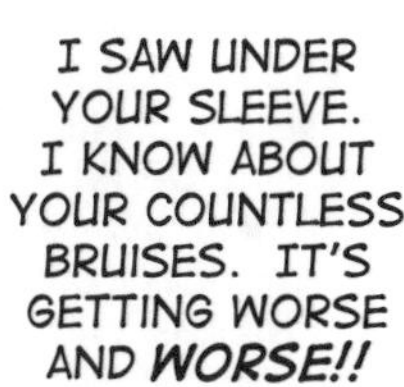

BUT I DESERVE IT. IT'S JUST AS MY HUSBAND SAYS.
"HOW LONG ARE YOU GOING TO KEEP ACTING THE KOBAYAKAWA PRINCESS? IN YOUR HEART YOU LOOK DOWN ON SOMEONE LIKE ME WHO COMES FROM LOWLY STOCK, DON'T YOU?" AND IT'S TRUE... I DO LOOK DOWN ON HIM.
HE'S VULGAR AND VAIN AND HAS MANY OTHER WOMEN BESIDES ME...IF I DIDN'T LOOK DOWN ON HIM, HOW COULD I GO ON?

OF COURSE IT SICKENS ME, TOO...BUT WHAT COULD I DO IF I LEFT?
EVERYTHING IS FINE AS LONG AS I PUT UP WITH IT...IF I DON'T, MY SON...MY CHIKAGE WILL SUFFER, TOO...!!

すっく!!
THUNK

MRS. SHINJO! LEAVE YOUR HOUSE IMMEDIATELY AND COME TO MY HOME! BRING YOUR SON, TOO!

DON'T WORRY! OUR HOUSEKEEPER JUST LEFT, SO WE HAVE A SPARE ROOM. IF THERE ARE ANY PROBLEMS WITH THE CUSTODY OF YOUR SON, I'LL INTRODUCE YOU TO A GOOD LAWYER!

WHAT?

B...BUT MRS. TACHIBANA, I...

THUMP!!

YOU CAN TELL SHE'S TACHIBANA'S MOTHER!!

IF YOU STAY THERE, SOONER OR LATER YOU'LL BE KILLED! WHAT WILL HAPPEN TO YOUR SON THEN?!

MOTHER...

I CAN'T...
I CAN'T LEAVE THIS HOUSE...! I'VE NEVER WORKED A DAY IN MY LIFE!

MOTHER ...

THAT'S RIGHT... NO MATTER HOW MUCH I MAY LOOK DOWN ON THEM, I CAN'T SUPPORT MYSELF OR THIS CHILD WITHOUT THE HELP OF THE SHINJO FAMILY.
THIS CHILD WHO IS STILL SUCH A BABY DESPITE HIS YEARS...LET HIM AT LEAST HAVE A LIFE WITHOUT MONEY WORRIES...

MOTHER.
IT'S OKAY, MOTHER -- I'M ALREADY A BIG BOY...I'M THE TALLEST IN MY CLASS.
I'LL BE BIGGER THAN FATHER SOON...THEN WE'LL BE OKAY WITHOUT HIM. I CAN TAKE FATHER'S PLACE.

SO PLEASE, MOTHER... DON'T BE HIT ANYMORE.

CHIKAGE!
I'M SORRY! I'M SORRY! I LIED... I WASN'T STAYING FOR YOUR SAKE... I WAS SCARED FOR MYSELF, TO BE WITHOUT MONEY!
LET'S LEAVE THIS HOUSE! LET'S LEAVE THIS HOUSE TOGETHER AND LIVE FOR OURSELVES...!!

PUFF
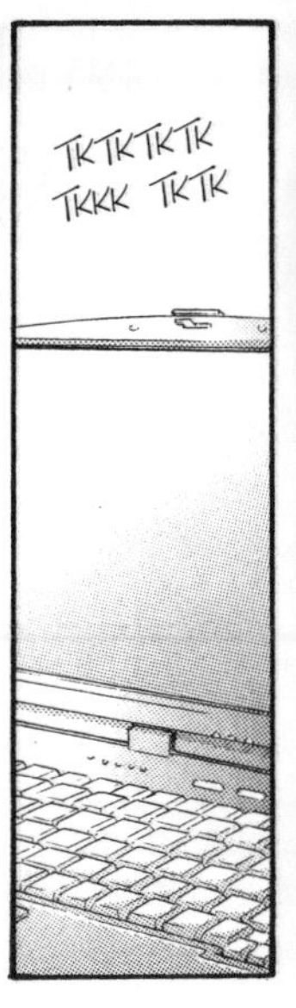
TKTKTKTK
TKKK TKTK

...
...!!
SCRATCH
SCRATCH
SCRATCH
SCRATCH!!

...
...

CLAK
CLAK
CLAK
CLAK
CLAK

URRGH...THIS WON'T HOLD TOGETHER AT ALL, DAMMIT...!
CREAK
MOMMY...

...
...
WHAT?

パタン
THUNK

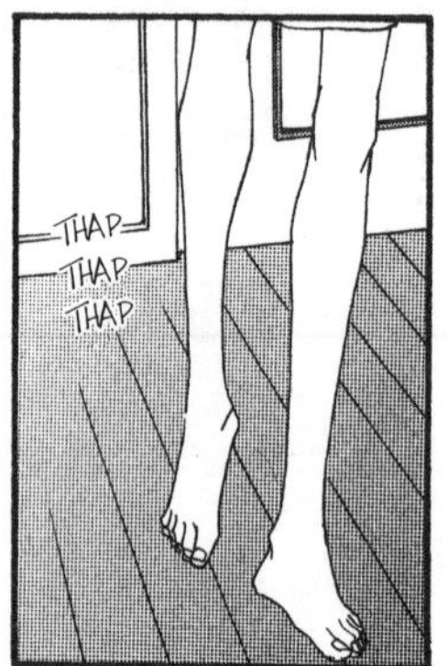
THAP
THAP
THAP

LEAN

SLAP

WHAT ARE YOU DOING?!

DON'T CLOY, YOU STUPID CHILD!

I...I'M HUNGRY.
LOOK IN THE FRIDGE! DON'T I ALWAYS TELL YOU TO MAKE SOMETHING YOURSELF?
B...BUT I WANT SOMETHING SWEET...

I...I WANT A CAKE OR SOMETHING!
A CAKE?!
WHAT A SPOILED BRAT! IF YOU WANT ONE SO BADLY, WHY DON'T YOU USE YOUR OWN ALLOWANCE AND GO BUY IT AT THE CONVENIENCE STORE?!

I...I WANT YOU TO BAKE ME ONE!
IMPOSSIBLE! DO YOU KNOW WHEN MY DEADLINE IS? IT'S TOMORROW... TOMORROW!! ANYWAY, I'M ALWAYS TELLING YOU NOT TO COME IN HERE WHEN I'M WORKING. NOW, GET OUT!

YOU...YOU ALWAYS SAY THAT AND THEN YOU ALWAYS GET YOUR NEXT JOB!
YOU USED TO BE NICER TO DEKO BEFORE, MOMMY...NOW YOU'RE JUST MAD ALL THE TIME! DEKO DOESN'T LIKE YOU NOW... I HATE YOU! I HOPE YOU DIE!

SMACK!!

YOU'RE LIVING OFF THE MONEY THAT I EARN WITH THIS JOB, AND YOU'RE TELLING ME TO *DIE? SHUT UP, YOU STUPID GIRL!!*
THEN WHY DON'T YOU LEAVE?!

GET OUT, GO ON! GO! GO!
SLAP
SLAP
SLAP
NO OO~!
GO!
SLAP
GO GO GO!!
SLAP

IF YOU DON'T LIKE IT, WHY DON'T YOU EARN YOUR OWN LIVING BY TURNING TRICKS OR FOOLING OLD MEN OR WHATEVER? *IDIOT!!*

THUD!!

CLOSED

COGNAC-FLAVORED CRÈME BRULÉE.

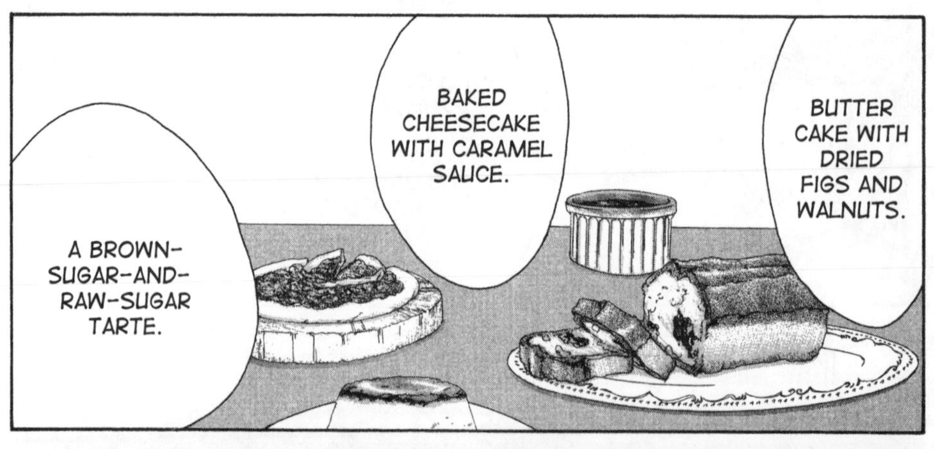
A BROWN-SUGAR-AND-RAW-SUGAR TARTE.
BAKED CHEESECAKE WITH CARAMEL SAUCE.
BUTTER CAKE WITH DRIED FIGS AND WALNUTS.

NOW, NOW...LET'S JUST TRY SOME, SHALL WE?

THEY'RE ALL JUST... BROWN...

EIJI...NO ELEGANCE... THERE'S ***NO ELEGANCE*** IN THE CAKES YOU MAKE...

IT'S JUST SUGAR IN THIS TARTE?

SH...***SHUT UP!*** I KNOW MY CAKES AREN'T PRETTY, BUT...!

OH?!
ON THE OUTSIDE IT LOOKS LIKE JUST AN ORDINARY PUDDING BUT WHEN YOU TAKE A BITE, IT TASTES OF FRANCE! IT'S THE POWER OF COGNAC!
IT'S DELICIOUS! EVEN THOUGH IT'S JUST SUGAR! AND IT SMELLS GOOD!
YES. A CHARACTERISTIC OF BROWN SUGAR IS THAT, WHEN BAKED, IT EMITS A RUM-LIKE AROMA.
... ...

KANDA.
THIS BUTTER CAKE...THE CONTRAST IN TEXTURE BETWEEN THE DRIED FIGS SOFTENED IN WHITE WINE AND THE CRUNCHINESS OF THE WALNUTS IS VERY GOOD.
THE CAKE ITSELF IS MOIST AND BUTTERY, TOO -- IT'S DELICIOUS. I'D LIKE TO MAKE THIS A REGULAR ITEM OF OURS ALMOST IMMEDIATELY.

THE OTHERS ARE VARIATIONS ON PROVINCIAL PASTRIES...THE RAW-SUGAR TARTE OF NORTHERN FRANCE, THE CRÈME AU COGNAC OF CHARENTE, THE GOAT-CHEESE CAKE OF CORSICA...BUT EACH ONE CLEARLY SHOWS YOUR PERSONAL CREATIVITY. I THINK THAT, WITH THE RIGHT SORT OF PROMOTION, THESE CAKES WILL BECOME REPEAT SELLERS.

BUT THERE'S STILL SOME ROOM FOR IMPROVEMENT IN THE COMBINATION OF INGREDIENTS AND DEGREE OF "DONENESS" IN BAKING...ALSO, REMEMBER THAT PRESENTATION CAN BE SIMPLE, BUT IT MUST ALSO BE STYLISH. GOOD LUCK!
YES!
CREAK
CHI...
OH? THIS IS GOOD. ONO'S FINALLY GOTTEN INTO THE "TRAINING" MENTALITY...

CHI...

DEKO!!

HUH?

W...WHAT'S WRONG, DEKO? SO LATE AT NIGHT...

PLEASE LET DEKO STAY AT CHI'S TONIGHT...

HERE, DEI-DEI. HAVE SOME COCOA.

WHAT'S WRONG? YOU LIKE IT, DON'T YOU? GO ON AND DRINK UP.

KEI-KEI...
YOUR FACE...
IT'S SCARY...
IT LOOKS
FUNNY...

QUIET!
IT'S NOT
SCARY OR
FUNNY-LOOKING!
IF YOU KEEP
SAYING THINGS
LIKE THAT...

WHAT'S THIS...?
WHAT'S
HAPPENING...?

SHE'S A
REALLY CUTE
LITTLE KID
THOUGH,
ISN'T SHE...

HEY!
LOOK
DEKO~!
I'M GONNA
SANDPAPER
YOU~!
EEEEK!
NOOO,
KEI-KEI~!!

M...M...
MR.CHIKAGE!
THAT GIRL...!!
OH!
ISN'T SHE
CUTE?
HER NAME IS
KAEDEKO.

OH! OH, OHHH... I GET IT! SHE'S THE DAUGHTER OF A RELATIVE OF TACHIBANA'S!
NOPE!
DIRECT
I DON'T REALLY CARE IF THE GEEZER'S ARRESTED FOR SOLICITING A MINOR, BUT WHAT'LL HAPPEN TO THIS STORE...?
PRRRRR

HM? SORRY, JUST A SEC. HELLO?
OH.

HOLD ON, I'LL CALL YOU RIGHT BACK.
OKAY, DEKO... YOU JUST DRINK YOUR COCOA WHILE IT'S HOT.
P!
?

CHIKAGE, YOU TAKE CARE OF DEKO. IT'S BEEN A WHILE FOR YOU TWO, HASN'T IT?
YES.

H...*HEY! TACHIBANA...! ABOUT THAT GIRL...!*
I'VE GOTTA TAKE CARE OF SOMETHING RIGHT NOW...I'LL TELL YOU LATER.

IS IT GOOD?

...

HM?

CLACK

CLIMB

ぺたぁ
SLAM!

CHI...
HMM...?
MOMMY...SHE USED TO HOLD DEKO LIKE THIS...SHE USED TO ROCK DEKO BACK AND FORTH LIKE CHI DOES...BUT NOW SHE DOESN'T ANYMORE...SO DEKO WENT UP TO MOMMY AND HUGGED HER.

BUT THEN MOMMY *HIT* DEKO.
I THINK MOMMY DOESN'T LOVE DEKO ANYMORE...

DEI-DEI.
WHEN YOU LOOK AT MOMMY, SHE LOOKS LIKE A GROWNUP TO YOU, DOESN'T SHE?

BUT EVEN YOUR MOMMY CAN BE TROUBLED...LIKE WHEN SHE'S WORKING REALLY HARD. GROWNUPS HAVE TIMES WHEN THEY WANT TO CLING TO SOMEBODY, TOO...JUST LIKE DEI-DEI DOES.

DID YOU KNOW THAT?

THEY DO...?
THAT'S RIGHT.
DEI-DEI... YOU'RE A BIG GIRL NOW.
SO WHEN YOU .SEE THAT YOUR MOMMY IS HAVING A TOUGH TIME, YOU HAVE TO ACT LIKE THE MOMMY-- FOR YOUR MOM THIS TIME.

EVEN THE MOST ADMIRABLE PEOPLE WHO CAN DO EVERYTHING... THEY HAVE TOUGH TIMES, TOO.

CHIKAGE!

"MY LORD?!"
"DON'T TELL... DON'T TELL...!"
"DON'T TELL ANYONE...!"

"I WON'T! I WON'T TELL ANYONE..."

OK?

OK.
DO YOU LIKE CAKE, DEI-DEI? DO YOU WANT SOMETHING TO EAT?
GOOD.
OK.

UNFORTUNATELY, WE'RE ALL SOLD OUT OF THE CAKES MADE BY OUR GENIUS PASTRY CHEF AND WE'VE ONLY GOT THESE BROWN, SORRY-LOOKING CAKES MADE BY OUR LOWLY APPRENTICE...BUT GO AHEAD -- YOU PICK WHICHEVER ONE YOU WANT.
MGGH!
DAMN YOU, GEEZER!
BEWIL-DERED!
THIS ONE ...
OHHH, THAT'S SUPPOSED TO BE SOME KIND OF CAKE WITH DRIED FIGS OR SOMETHING, I DON'T REALLY KNOW.

IT'S GOOD!

R...REALLY?! YOU REALLY THINK IT'S GOOD?!
DID YOU MAKE THIS, MISTER? IT'S JUST LIKE MY MOMMY'S CAKE!

MMM... IT'S GOOD...!

SHE'S CUUUTE!
ISN'T SHE?! ISN'T SHE?!
I...I FEEL LEFT OUT...
SLAM!

KAEDEKO!!

OH, HEY. YOU TOOK YOUR TIME, SAKURAKO.
THIS STORE IS TOO HARD TO FIND, KEIICHIRO!

YOU IDIOT DAUGHTER! YOU TOOK MONEY FROM MY WALLET FOR A TAXI, DIDN'T YOU!
YOU'RE USUALLY SO SLOW, BUT SMART ENOUGH FOR SOMETHING LIKE THIS!
WAAAAH~!
MISS SAKURAKO, PLEASE DON'T HIT HER!

WHAT, CHIKAGE... SUDDENLY FEELING FATHERLY AFTER ALL THIS TIME?!

T...
TACHIBANA...?!
WHO... IS WHO'S...?
...FATHER...?!
YEAH, YOU SEE...

THIS...

...IS THIS ONE'S...

...FATHER ...?!

WHAT A SHOCK...SO, HE WAS SEXUALLY ACTIVE AFTER ALL...

HE ACTUALLY KNEW HOW TO MAKE CHILDREN...

AND JUST FOR THE RECORD, I'VE GOT A PERFECTLY GOOD RELATIONSHIP WITH A DIFFERENT MAN RIGHT NOW.

CHIK

FOOF
I WAS FEELING PRETTY ANXIOUS BACK THEN.

SURE I WENT THROUGH A LOT OF MEN, BUT WHEN IT CAME TO MARRIAGE...ONE THING LED TO ANOTHER. I WON THE NAOKI AWARD, GOT BUSIER... AND BEFORE I KNEW IT, I WAS APPROACHING FORTY.
HUH?! *THE NAOKI AWARD?!*
U...UM...THEN COULD IT BE THAT YOU'RE SAKURAKO SAKAKI, THE NOVELIST?! THE AUTHOR OF **"AFTERGLOW"?!**

OH, SO YOU READ THAT, DID YOU.
THE ONE WHERE THE SEX SCENES BETWEEN THE MAN AND WOMAN WERE SO GRAPHIC AND RAW THAT I COULDN'T FINISH IT...
?
BUT I ALWAYS WANTED TO HAVE A CHILD. SO JUST WHEN I WAS THINKING THAT ANY MAN WOULD DO AS LONG AS HE HAD SPERM, I WAS INVITED BY A MUTUAL FRIEND OF KEIICHIRO'S TO THE TACHIBANA FAMILY'S TRADITIONAL NEW YEAR'S PARTY, AND THAT'S WHERE I MET CHIKAGE.

ばしゃー
SPLOOSH!

WHAT'S GOING ON?! WHAT IDIOT THREW CHAMPAGNE OVER MY HEAD?!
I...I'M ***SO*** SORRY!

HE DOESN'T LOOK VERY BRIGHT, BUT HE DOES LOOK LIKE HE'S GOT SOME LIVELY SPERM...

I'M SORRY...

WITH MY BRAINS AND CHIKAGE'S LOOKS, DON'T YOU THINK OUR CHILD WOULD BE THE BEST?! OF COURSE THERE WAS THE CHANCE THAT THE RESULT COULD BE THE EXACT OPPOSITE, BUT...
THINK ABOUT IT!
SO CRUDE...
...
...

AND THE RESULT?

JUST LIKE CHIKAGE, BOTH INSIDE AND OUT.
one-win-one-loss ?
NO BRAINS EITHER...

I SWEAR! SHE'S IN FOURTH GRADE AND SHE STILL CAN'T RECITE HER NINE-TIMES TABLES!

FOURTH GRADE?!
EIJI...
ARE YOU REALLY THAT TALL?
BUT ...HER HEIGHT! HER CHEST!!
ONO...
UH-HUH. THE TALLEST IN MY CLASS.
WELL, I MEAN... SHE *IS* CHIKAGE'S KID, SO...
TACHI-BANA...

IMAGINE SUDDENLY BEING CLAMBERED ON BY THAT 5-FOOT-2, 106-POUND GIRL... IT'S NO JOKE. THANKS TO THAT, MY ALREADY BAD BACK HAS GOTTEN WORSE...

WHAT?

OOPS!

MISS SAKURAKO, WHY DIDN'T YOU TELL DEKO ABOUT THAT?
SAKURAKO! YOUR HERNIA IS NOT GONNA GO AWAY...SO YOU'VE GOT TO GET A LITTLE EXERCISE, AT LEAST!
QUIET!!

...
MOMMY... YOU'RE ILL?

...
...

I DIDN'T WANT HER TO WORRY, THAT'S ALL!

...
...
スーパ
スパッ
スパッ
スパッ
PUFF
PUFF
PUFF
PUFF

COME ON -- WE'RE GOING HOME, KAEDEKO!
I CAN AT LEAST HOLD YOUR HAND. MY DEADLINE IS TOMORROW, YOU KNOW! ***HURRY UP!***

SIZZZ

DAH!!
IN OUR ANTIQUE!!

SEE YOU AGAIN, DEI-DEI.

BYE BYE, CHI.

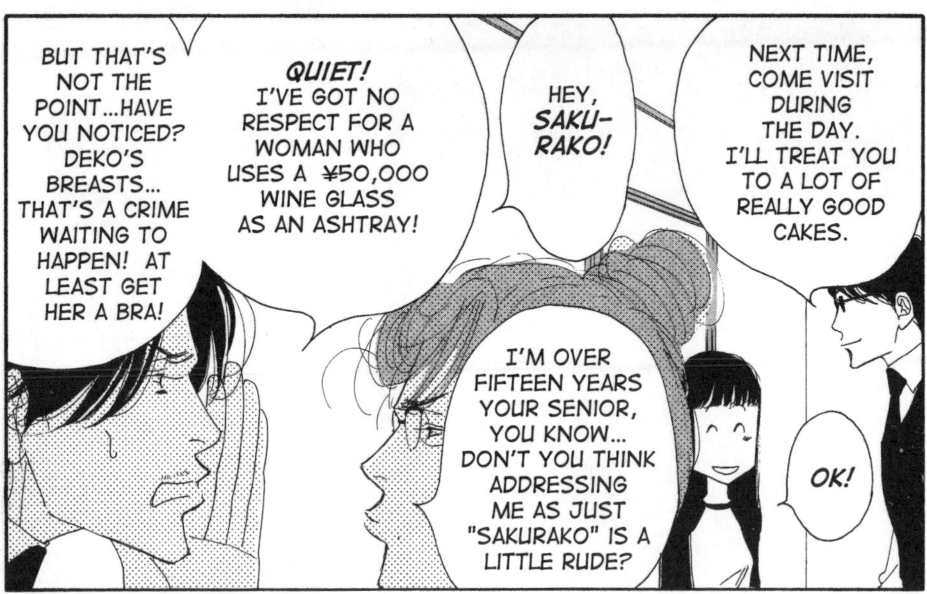
NEXT TIME, COME VISIT DURING THE DAY. I'LL TREAT YOU TO A LOT OF REALLY GOOD CAKES.
OK!
HEY, SAKU-RAKO!
I'M OVER FIFTEEN YEARS YOUR SENIOR, YOU KNOW... DON'T YOU THINK ADDRESSING ME AS JUST "SAKURAKO" IS A LITTLE RUDE?
QUIET! I'VE GOT NO RESPECT FOR A WOMAN WHO USES A ¥50,000 WINE GLASS AS AN ASHTRAY!
BUT THAT'S NOT THE POINT...HAVE YOU NOTICED? DEKO'S BREASTS... THAT'S A CRIME WAITING TO HAPPEN! AT LEAST GET HER A BRA!

WHAAAT? IT'S TOO MUCH TROUBLE! SHE'S ONLY GOING TO GET BIGGER. IT CAN WAIT.
AND YOU CALL YOURSELF A MOTHER?! IT'S FOR POOR DEKO'S SAKE!
...

HOW IS SHE "POOR"?! AND ANYWAY, WHEN SHE BLOODIED UP HER SHORTS BECAUSE HER PERIOD STARTED, THE SCHOOL PROMPTLY GAVE HER A CHANGE OF UNDERWEAR AND A SANITARY NAPKIN. THE SCHOOLS TAKE CARE OF EVERYTHING NOWADAYS, YOU KNOW.

MASTER?! ARE YOU OKAY, MASTER?!
WHY YOU...!!
NO! KEI-KEI!!
S...SORRY... JUST FEELING A LITTLE FAINT...
SO CRUDE...

DON'T YELL AT MOMMY! IF YOU'RE MEAN TO MOMMY, DEKO WILL NEVER FORGIVE YOU, KEI-KEI!

I THINK MISS SAKURAKO REALLY, REALLY, DESPERATELY WANTED A CHILD BACK THEN.
WATER, MASTER!
THANK YOU...

SOB!

SAKURAKO! DID YOU JUST HEAR THAT?! HOW THOUGHTFUL SHE IS OF HER MOTHER?!
YOU JUST DON'T GET IT, DO YOU? I'M THE ONE THAT RAISED HER TO BE THAT WAY!!
SQUEEZE...

PLEASE!
I NEED YOU TO SLEEP WITH ME! I WANT TO HAVE A CHILD...BUT I DON'T HAVE MUCH TIME LEFT! PLEASE...!

BUT WOULD SOMEONE NORMALLY AGREE TO HELP OUT IN THAT TYPE OF SITUA-TION?!

SHE GREW UP IN A PRETTY HARSH FAMILY ENVIRONMENT, AND THAT'S PROBABLY WHAT MADE HER WANT HER OWN FAMILY SO BADLY. SHE WAS ALSO GOING THROUGH SOME PERSONAL PROBLEMS AT THE TIME. SHE SEEMED DESPERATE -- LIKE SHE WAS UP AGAINST THE WALL.

CHIKAGE LOVES CHILDREN MORE THAN ANYONE, BUT HE REALIZED HE COULDN'T BE A GOOD FATHER... AND EVEN KNOWING THAT HE WOULDN'T BE ABLE TO LIVE WITH HIS OWN CHILD, HE STILL AGREED TO HELP SAKURAKO CONCEIVE.

IF IT'S SOMETHING HE'S CAPABLE OF, CHIKAGE ALWAYS AGREES TO HELP.
OH! I KNOW...OLDER WOMEN LIKE THAT ARE GOOD IN BED, AREN'T THEY? I GETCHA.
WAAAH~! EVERY-ONE, STOP~!
AND IT FELT REALLY GOOD...♡
BECAUSE THERE'S SO LITTLE THAT HE IS CAPABLE OF...

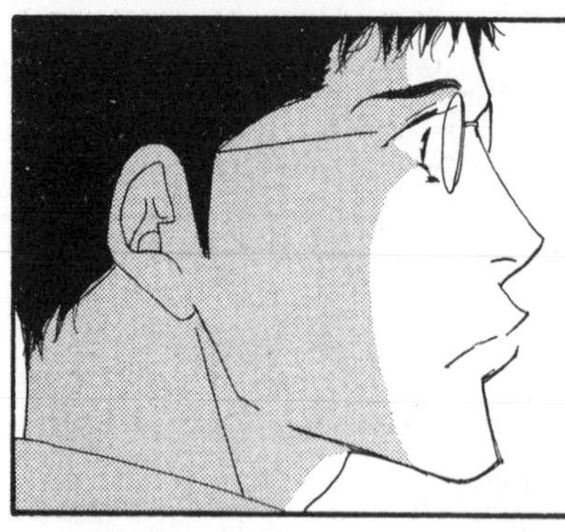
THAT'S THE KIND OF GUY HE IS.
AND WHEN SAKURAKO WOULD CAPRICIOUSLY SHOW UP WITH THE BABY, UPSET BECAUSE SHE COULDN'T HANDLE THINGS, CHIKAGE ALWAYS TOOK OVER DEKO'S CARE WITHOUT A SINGLE COMPLAINT.

OH...
A MAN WHO CAN EVEN BABY-SIT!!
IT'S LIKE DEKO IS HALF MY KID, TOO.
THOUGH, OF COURSE, I WAS THE ONE WHO DID ALL THE ACTUAL LOOKING-AFTER!
WILL WONDERS NEVER CEASE!
?

HEY, I TOLD YOU NOT TO LEAN ON ME! YOU'RE HEAVY!
HEE HEE HEE

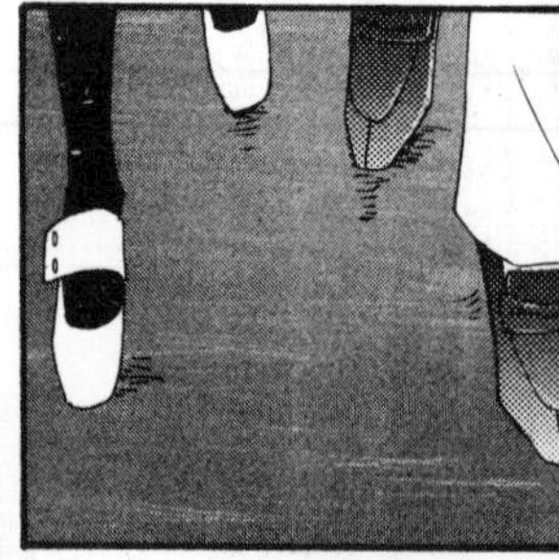

SLIP

AFTER I'VE MET MY DEADLINE, SHALL I MAKE YOU THAT BUTTER CAKE WITH PEARS I MADE BEFORE?
HEY.

NO, IT'S OKAY.

BUT INSTEAD, TEACH DEKO HOW TO MAKE THAT CAKE, OKAY?
DEKO IS ALREADY IN THE FOURTH GRADE...SO NOW IT'S DEKO'S TURN TO MAKE MOMMY A CAKE.

OHH! CHILDREN CAN BE SO CUTE! OHH!
HEE HEE!
OHHH!
I KNEW IT...I KNEW I'D BE GLAD THAT I HAD A CHILD!

REALLY GLAD.

OH, THAT'S RIGHT. DO YOU WANT A BRA PRETTY SOON? AFTER THE DEADLINE I CAN GO WITH YOU TO BUY ONE.
HUUUH? NOOO... I DON'T NEED ONE. I'LL JUST GET BIGGER. IT'S TOO MUCH TROUBLE.
SO SHE DOES TAKE AFTER ME IN SOME WAYS AFTER ALL.

CONTINUED TO VOLUME 4

WELL! NOW THAT THE WEDDING IS OVER WITH...
I'LL TREAT YOU GUYS TO DINNER! LET'S HAVE SUSHI! THERE'S THIS REALLY GOOD PLACE CLOSE BY...
MY LORD! I CAN'T EAT SUSHI UNLESS I TAKE OUT ALL THE WASABI!
BLECH! I HATE RAW FOOD!!

THEN HOW ABOUT TABLETOP BARBEQUE?! YOU GUYS DON'T HAVE ANY PROBLEM WITH MEAT, RIGHT? THERE'S THIS REALLY GOOD PLACE CLOSE BY...
HUH?! NO BARBEQUE! I JUST BOUGHT THIS NEW JACKET - IT'LL GET ALL SMELLY!

SO, WE END UP AT A FAMILY RESTAURANT...
GOOD WORK TODAY!
ting!
ICE TEA...
SODA FLOAT...
ORANGE JUICE...
BEER...

YOU GUYS! DON'T YOU GUYS HAVE ANY APPETITE FOR DELICACIES?! LIKE THE FIRM DORSAL MEAT OF FLOUNDER?! FLUFFY STEWED EEL?! CREAMY SEA URCHIN?!
SUPER JUICY KALBI WITH THE BONE LEFT IN?! SALTED TONGUE OR SKEWERED LIVER OR BIBIMBAP COOKED ON HOT STONE?!
LET'S DIG IN! ♥
LET'S DIG IN! ♥

I LOVE MACARONI AU GRATIN! ♥
YOU LUCKED OUT, KANDA.
......
YAAY, SALISBURY STEAK! ♥

WHEN MAKING DINNER PLANS, BE SURE TO MAKE THEM WITH FRIENDS WHO SHARE YOUR TASTES.

Café Kichijouji de 1
"Irrasshai!"
"Welcome!" to the hilarious and most unruly café in all of Kichijouji...
...With its charming staff of five who's largely conflicting personalities usually result in even larger repair bills!
A new manga based on the popular Japanese Radio Drama!
DMP
DIGITAL MANGA PUBLISHING
A New Wave of Manga
Cafe KICHIJOUJI DE © KYOKO NEGISHI/ YUKI MIYAMOTO 2001.
Originally published in Japan in 2001 by SHINSHOKAN CO., LTD.

YELLOW

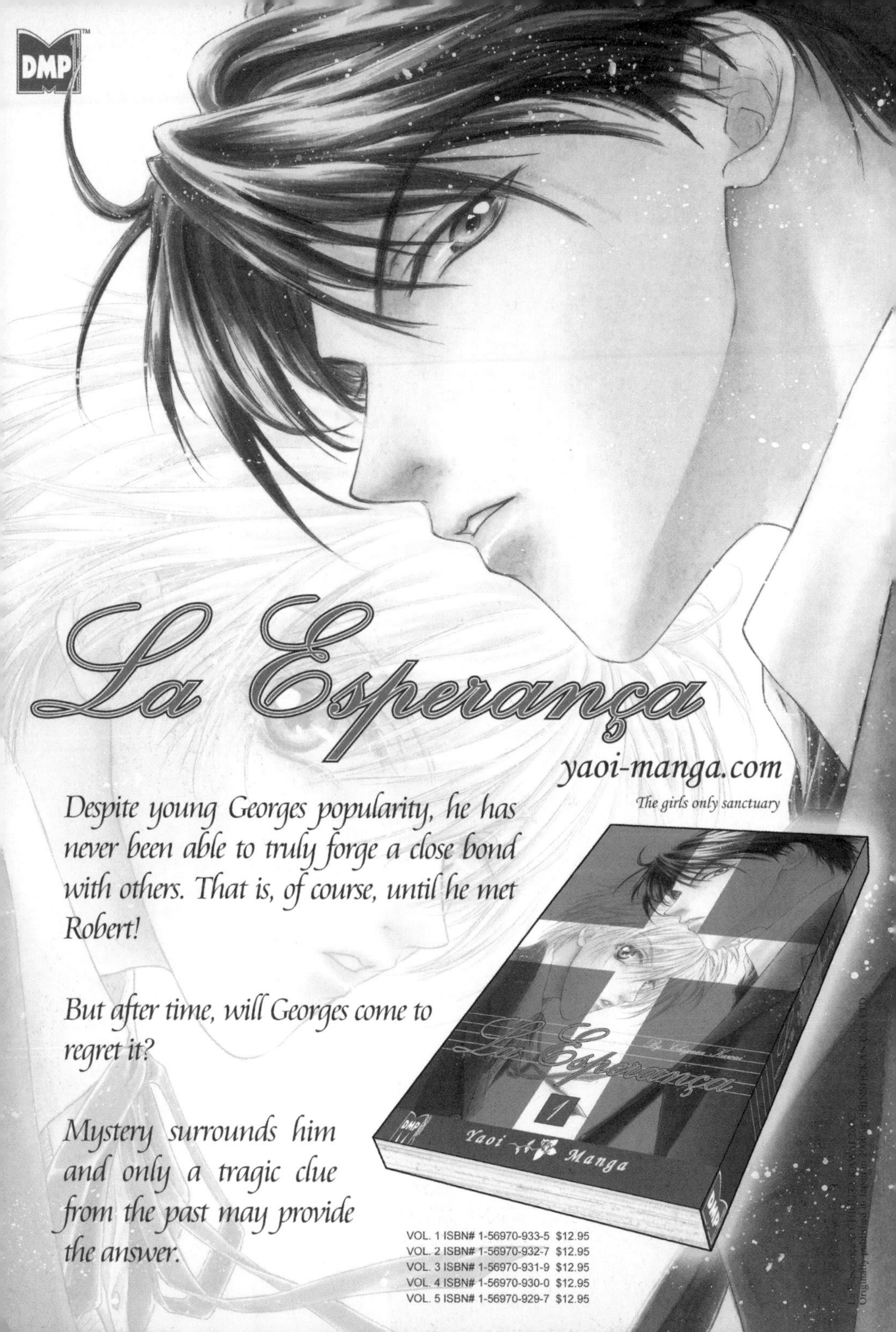

DMP
La Esperança
yaoi-manga.com
The girls only sanctuary
Despite young Georges popularity, he has never been able to truly forge a close bond with others. That is, of course, until he met Robert!
But after time, will Georges come to regret it?
Mystery surrounds him and only a tragic clue from the past may provide the answer.
La Esperança
1
Yaoi Manga
VOL. 1 ISBN# 1-56970-933-5 $12.95
VOL. 2 ISBN# 1-56970-932-7 $12.95
VOL. 3 ISBN# 1-56970-931-9 $12.95
VOL. 4 ISBN# 1-56970-930-0 $12.95
VOL. 5 ISBN# 1-56970-929-7 $12.95

DMP
Kimi Shiruya-
Dost thou Know?
When Katsuomi and Tsurugi's wooden swords collide, sparks will fly, but as pride gets in the way of love, Tsurugi's brother Saya will profess his love to Katsuomi...
...Will jealousy drive Tsurugi to battle it out with Katsuomi one last time?
ISBN# 1-56970-934-3 $12.95
yaoi-manga.com
The girls only sanctuary
KIMI SHIRUYA- Dost Thou Know? © SATORU ISHIHARA 2003.
Originally published in Japan in 2003 by SHINSHOKAN CO., LTD.

STOP

This is the back of the book! Start from the other side.

***NATIVE MANGA* readers read manga from *right to left*.**

1
2
3
1
2
3
4
5
6
5
4
7
8
6

If you run into our ***Native Manga*** *logo on any of our books... you'll know that this manga is published in it's true original native Japanese right to left reading format, as it was intended. Turn to the other side of the book and start reading from right to left, top to bottom.*

Follow the diagram to see how its done.
Surf's Up!

NATIVE MANGA
READ RIGHT TO LEFT